Tackling Jim Crow

ALSO BY ALAN H. LEVY

*Rube Waddell: The Zany, Brilliant Life
of a Strikeout Artist*
(McFarland, 2000)

Tackling Jim Crow

Racial Segregation in Professional Football

by ALAN H. LEVY

McFarland & Company, Inc., Publishers
Jefferson, North Carolina, and London

The photographs in this book are used with the permission of the Pro Football Hall of Fame, Canton, Ohio.

LIBRARY OF CONGRESS ONLINE CATALOG DATA

Levy, Alan H.
    Tackling Jim Crow : racial segregation in professional football / by Alan H. Levy.
        p.   cm.
    Includes bibliographical references and index.

    ISBN 0-7864-1597-5 (softcover : 50# alkaline paper)

    1. Football—Social aspects—United States—History.
    2. Discrimination in sports—United States—History.
    3. African American football players—History.
    4. National Football League—History.   I. Title.

GV943.9.S64 L48   2003
796.332'0896'073—dc21   2003005735

British Library cataloguing data are available

Manufactured in the United States of America

Cover art © 2003 PicturesNow.com

McFarland & Company, Inc., Publishers
  Box 611, Jefferson, North Carolina 28640
    www.mcfarlandpub.com

This book is dedicated to the memory
of those who fought for racial integration
in professional sports—for all you endured.

Contents

Introduction

Any study of culture and politics in America has to consider matters of race. So many of America's collective anxieties that have been conquered, and at least as many still unconquered, connect to issues of race. This has been so since the advent of slavery and the many accompanying psychic contortions that Americans performed somehow to reconcile themselves to the history of their inhumane habits which lay in dissonance both to their political ideals of democracy and to the better angels of their nature. The heritage of racism has permeated virtually everywhere.

As issues of race have permeated so many features of the national culture, a myriad of narratives and analytical paradigms have served as useful means through which these issues have been studied. Some modes of inquiry involved examinations of the lives of famous as well as of ordinary individuals. Some approaches involve public policy issues, legal issues, and political ideologies. Other studies concerned the work of people in highly visible areas of human activity.

Examinations of activities in such visible endeavors as music, theater, literature, the arts, and sports can serve to enliven analyses of ways in which race issues have manifested themselves in America's history. This is especially important in regard to the question of how racial attitudes have affected people, and in turn how others who witness such attitudes have themselves been affected.

In visible fields like music, the arts, and sports, analyses of race and human attainment always mix with questions of quality. As the quality of achievement in any field of endeavor can usually be judged regardless of the race of the individuals involved, the injustices of racial prejudice come crashing forth when people of demonstrable quality are held back or when others are allowed to advance for reasons that have more to do with who they are rather than what they do. Examples here are sadly voluminous: Paul Robeson, for one, was

1

denied entry, after auditioning, for a men's chorus at Rutgers; Miles Davis was not allowed to play trumpet in his high school band. Neither was considered good enough! (Robeson was told that a "pitch problem" would make him "stick out.") Surrounding such stories of denial come different questions as to styles of expression and creativity that may be linked to race, as well as to such other matters as age, gender, region, class, and historical era. The history of racial issues in many fields thus can center on different subjects, with approaches that involve highly differentiated sorts of questions: How, for example, has racial consciousness held many back despite their extraordinary ability; how has race characterized the nature of the expressions in some fields of endeavor? There can be tension when one tries to cover both issues simultaneously.

In the fields of music, the arts, and entertainment, the tensions between racially defined creativity and the quest for respect regardless of race have been strong, as some zealously regard racial identity as essential to the substance of their work. In the area of sports, the simple matter of quality, regardless of race, has been predominant. If there are modes and manners of expression that are linked to race which tinge the work of players in a particular game, most thoughtful people prefer simply to let such dynamics take whatever courses they will, with quality remaining the key in the final analysis. A chief historical dynamic in the history of African Americans and other minorities in American sports has been that simple quality has all too often not been allowed to speak for itself.

In individual sports there has always been the undeniable point that when quality has been in contention, one must simply let the individuals in question contest one another. Track and field events have always been obvious cases in point. Given the quantifiable nature of the results, when racial barriers prevented certain people from competing, victories and records set under such circumstances have had a certain hollowness, especially when champions in subsequent, less-prejudiced eras achieve demonstrably superior results.

Boxing is another obvious example. For years laws and customs prevented African American boxers from competing with Anglos. Despite this, many fans could not be dissuaded from the simple point that there was obviously one simple way to settle the question of who's the better of any pair of pugilists—put the two of them in the ring. At various times, observers and writers did note that some champion boxers refused to contest challengers on the basis of race. John L. Sullivan, for example, while universally recognized as heavyweight champion in the late nineteenth century, did explicitly "draw the color line" (the genteel phrase of the day used to denote a refusal to fight blacks). Reporters at the time were hardly outraged by this, but they did comment on it. Sullivan refused, for example, to box the Australian fighter Peter Jackson, by all accounts a more than worthy challenger. Sullivan's refusal came solely because Jackson was black. Reporters did not vilify Sullivan for his refusal, as many would have in later generations, but his drawing of a "racial line" did not go unnoted.

Jack Johnson was, of course, the most famous black boxer of the early twentieth century, and he was denied many opportunities to fight for championships. If he fought a white man and did not knock him out, the judges would never award Johnson a decision. Everyone in the fight business in the early twentieth century knew how good Johnson was, but no one would give him a title shot. He was only able to get one chance at the heavyweight championship, and that came through unusual and fortuitous perseverance. The man who held the crown before him, Canadian Tommy Burns, had been ducking Johnson for several months. Burns went on a tour of Australia, and Johnson simply trailed him down there. As much out of futility and exhaustion, as with having few others to fight, Burns relented and gave Johnson a chance while both were in Australia. Johnson made the most of it, to say the least, and took the title. Whether Burns, being Canadian, did not feel bound by quite the same prejudices as his American counterparts is not fully known, but the fight would most certainly have never occurred in the United States.

American contemporaries, notably Jim Jeffries, were most severe in their racist convictions. While champion, Jeffries absolutely refused to face Johnson, and only agreed to fight him after Johnson had seized the crown. Jeffries was incensed and felt obliged to try to take back the title. He came out of retirement to do so. Despite the counsel of many boxing people, he scheduled no tune-up fights beforehand, and on July 4, 1910, he lost decisively to his hated opponent. At the fight, even avowedly racist reporters such as writer Jack London (who had coined the phrase "the great white hope" in regard to Jeffries and his fight with Johnson) acknowledged that Johnson had thoroughly bested the former champion. "The colored man," noted London, "showed no yellow." Despite such begrudging acknowledgments, however, the successes of Johnson eroded no social barriers; indeed, because of Johnson's successes and because of his particularly defiant manner (especially his marriage to a white woman), white recalcitrance over racial matters in early twentieth-century America generally deepened. In many states, theater owners could be arrested merely for showing films of Johnson fighting.

The obstacles of race lay everywhere in the sport of boxing and continued through the century. In the 1920s, Jack Dempsey regularly "drew the color line." Even as late as the 1970s, a white heavyweight contender, Jerry Quarry, received far more big money fights and title shots than many equals of his era because of his race. This was something Quarry himself freely admitted. Still, though, the boxing ring has always been the obvious example to all fans that quality can be proven one way or the other simply by putting two men in the ring and seeing who wins.

With team sports, in contrast, justifications in favor of segregation always played up allegedly more complicated issues of team dynamics. Here nervously driven, unspecific euphemisms have always spewed forth—how disruptive the race question could be to the effectiveness of a team, how African Americans lacked "some of the essentials" (to use former Los Angeles Dodgers' administrator Al Campanis's infamous 1987 phrase) for the team sport in question. In professional team sports there was also, among management, the fear-driven issue that the appearance of African Americans would hurt gate receipts. Of course, for decades there was never any proof of this, as integration had never been tested, but such lack of evidence was not important when all the team owners shared the very same fears and prejudices of the people of their times and willingly seized upon such rationale. As a result, while some individual sports like boxing and track saw an occasional glimmer of a crack in the racial walls, major team sports remained lily white. Though Jesse Owens, Joe Louis, and Henry Armstrong faced severely racist obstacles when they were first making their marks, baseball, football, and basketball were still strictly segregated, and the black athletes in those sports had no chance for the successes that Owens, Louis, and Armstrong earned.

When racial barriers began to fall in the major team sports, the political and social implications were enormous. The story of Jackie Robinson and the integration of major league baseball is the most famous tale of racial integration in American sports. Indeed it was, perhaps, a more significant part of Jim Crow's post World War II demise than any other single event. It was certainly at least as important as the integration of the U.S. Armed Forces in 1947, and may have been as psychologically significant as the Brown v. Board of Education Decision of 1954.

The Robinson story involved a confrontation of all the old barriers in law, custom, and sensibility among white Americans. Without question, the Robinson story is the most important saga in regard to the issue of race and sports in American history. The issue involved not just an individual but a team. A victorious African-American boxer could be regarded as a single figure standing against the white world. On a team, a successful African-American player compelled fuller recognition, for some whites had to be on his side, at least in one respect. Their team success showed that integration could work, something a successful boxer or sprinter could not as easily imply.

In the early-to-mid twentieth century, among all individual and team sports, baseball was *the* sport of the United States. News about Jackie Robinson's breaking of the color line thus reverberated into virtually every corner of American society. The changes in baseball did not merely reflect broader social changes occurring in America, they actually led them and helped hasten them. No other sport of the day could have such an impact in America.

It was not just in the world of sports but in a myriad of institutions and in American law that Jim Crow was beginning to crumble in post–World War II America. Though Jackie Robinson and the breaking of the racial barrier in baseball was unquestionably the most important part of the athletic world's contribution to this demise of Jim Crow, other sports followed similar patterns and made significant contributions too. Professional football, for example, although it did not hold nearly the same stature as major league baseball in 1940s America, also witnessed a breaking of the color line. Its saga, from the game's earliest days into the tortured history of segregation and desegregation, is an undertold one, but it too contributed to the climate that lay in back of the decay of segregation in America in the 1940s and 1950s. As in other walks of life, athletic and otherwise, this was a long and very hard struggle. In subsequent decades, as professional football grew in stature in America, the often difficult struggles of African Americans in their individual and collective successes in the game played significant roles in the nation's general struggles against its history of racial injustice.

One

The Early Days of Integration

While most people believe that Jackie Robinson was the first African American to play major league baseball, many a baseball trivia buff will eagerly point out that African Americans did play professional baseball during its infant days of the late nineteenth century. In 1872 J.W. Bud Fowler played for Evansville, Indiana. In 1884 Moses "Fleet" Walker and his brother Weldy played for Toledo. Both Evansville and Toledo were part of the American Association, then a major league, equal to the National League. In the 1880s Walker and a few other African Americans dotted the rosters of major league teams. It was towards the end of that decade that owners began to feel pressure along racial lines. By 1890, the popularity of professional baseball was clearly on the rise. As a spectator sport, it had previously been largely the purview of the leisure classes who had the afternoon time to watch. But the game was gaining appeal among the urban working classes. American cities were growing rapidly, and by the late 1880s sheer population growth yielded sufficient numbers of workers, who were either laid off or putting in work shifts at hours other than game time, to form increasingly sizable cores of fan support. Baseball owners were aware of the intense racial hatreds that existed among the working classes, hatreds stemming from simple racism as well as from historical antagonisms. Knowing the feelings out among the fans, baseball team owners began to make adjustments. Most richer people of the day were no less racist in their sensibilities, but they could view players, white or black, in a condescending light, much like a worker or a servant. While the wealthy then held as many prejudices as white laborers, the pattern of identification with athletes involved different social and psychological dynamics among the working classes. Laborers more readily regarded ballplayers as one of their own. With layoffs

7

always looming, furthermore, the thought of a black player holding onto a job while a white player/worker went unemployed brought to mind a hated practice of factories using blacks as strike breakers. With such social and psychological dynamics at work, baseball team owners witnessed venom against black players among laborers attending games. Comprehending this, owners consciously decided to cater to their growing customer base.

Not coincidentally, as leaders of sports teams were feeling the pressure to segregate, the laws of the land were changing to accommodate rising sentiments about race. The laws of the Reconstruction Era which banned racial discrimination and which were, at least in theory, still on the books, were all being struck down. States were given preeminence in deciding their own affairs; so, for example, the Civil Rights act of 1875 was voided. Left on their own, states and localities, which had already established local customs of racial discrimination, began to construct the network of Jim Crow barriers that came to encompass virtually all meaningful areas of social, economic, and political life. The courts struck down various local laws which augured against racial discrimination. And, most famously, when rising formal discriminatory strictures were challenged in the 1896 case of Plessy versus Ferguson, the Supreme Court validated virtually all segregation with their infamous declaration of the wisdom of "separate but equal" facilities. Racist efforts of employers, from steel mills to sports teams, were thus right in step with the rising institutionalized prejudices of the day.

The baseball world of the 1890s was expanding and growing more corporate. With the growth and incorporation, the game's leaders also became more concerned about propriety, fan interest, public relations and gate receipts. Very much following the growth of Jim Crow in the late nineteenth and early twentieth century, baseball became a consciously segregated enterprise, despite the clearly demonstrated skills of African Americans. The few African Americans in the game were eased out. No new African American talent was given an opportunity. Reporters who had previously written of a "talented dark-skinned receiver" were penning phrases like "that N_____ catcher."[1] Baseball segregated itself, and subsequent maverick attempts to recruit talented African Americans always failed. John McGraw, for example, manager of the New York Giants from 1902 to 1932, tried many times to sneak African Americans into his team. He usually tried to claim they were "Cuban," but he was always unsuccessful. (Knowing of his many efforts at utilizing African American talent, various African American newspapers praised McGraw with great affection upon his retirement.)[2]

When professional baseball nearly died from the betting scandals over the 1919 World Series, owners turned to the idea of creating an office of high commissioner. Inventing this new office, owners gave the figure extraordinary powers which could not be challenged, especially after 1922 when the United States Supreme Court, with rather dubious logic, gave baseball a special exemption from anti-trust. The man the baseball owners chose, Judge Kennesaw Mountain Landis, was a man who had built a reputation for allegedly high moral standards through the (not always scrupulous) intensity with which he had convicted accused German and Communist sympathizers in 1917, 1918, and 1919. (He was also the judge who had convicted boxer Jack Johnson, in effect, for sleeping with his own wife.) Landis loved the power of such situations as baseball offered him. Indeed, the only other sensibility within him which approached the intensity of his affection for power was his unalterable racism. Thus, as long as Judge Landis was in charge, baseball's color line was never going to be crossed. And it would not be until after Landis died.

Though both the timing and sequence of events were different, football followed a similar pattern to baseball in regard to the beginning and end of racial segregation. In its infant days of the late nineteenth and early twentieth century, professional football like baseball, was slightly open in regard to race. Then, with growth and profits and its corporate structure formalizing, it grew more explicitly segregated. This growth and emerging profitability did not occur in football, however, until the 1920s and '30s. Back in the 1880s when baseball was successfully implanting itself in the public mind and becoming the game of choice of virtually every boy in the land, football barely existed, and what did exist was a far cry from the game that grew in the mid-twentieth century. The story of the vicissitudes of Jim Crow on the gridiron then involved different patterns and chronology.

Before 1900, organized American football was not played much outside of a few colleges and athletic clubs. The rules of the game were also in a constant state of flux. When Princeton played Rutgers in 1869, the first acknowledged college football game in the nation, there were 25 players on each side, and the goal posts were 20 feet wide. The value of various scores—touchdowns, conversions, field goals, safeties—was indefinite. Before 1882 there was no ten-yard, or any other distance required to be completed in four downs. Indeed, there was no set number of downs (or "tries," the more common term of the day taken from rugby). A team relinquished possession of the ball only when it scored, fumbled, or chose to kick away. In 1882 the rules were changed, requiring a team to gain five yards (or lose ten) in three tries or give up the ball. (Ten yards in four downs was not the rule until 1912.) The number of players on a side was reduced from 25 to 15, and later to 11. The value of various scores went through a series of changes, with the 6, 3, 2, and 1 point values of the various scores of today's game not finally in place until 1909.

Perhaps even more significant than the issues of field dimensions, downs, and points, a significant set of rule changes came to the game in 1905. Before then, football was hellishly rough, and this was a major reason for the game's limited appeal. Prior to 1905, many an autumn week would pass with a notice or two in the papers of a young man dying in a football game. With rhetorical help from none less than President Theodore Roosevelt, the game's scions met and abolished some of football's dangerous tactics. Chief among the changes to cut down on injuries and deaths was the new rule that at least six offensive players had to line up on the line of scrimmage. This removed from the game murderous plays like the infamous "flying wedge," in which an entire team could start a considerable distance back from the line of scrimmage, run en masse, gather momentum uncontested, and ram through helpless defendants, somewhat like today's kick-off teams, who, not coincidentally, continue to have the highest injury rates of any squad in the modern game. With modern kick teams, sometimes fittingly called "suicide squads," the defensive team can at least move at the opposition with equal force. Before 1905, the defensive players had to stand at the line and take the hits; though with almost everyone playing both offense and defense, the defense always got their opportunity to return the blows. When one considers such plays occurring with the era's players wearing few pads and no helmets, the dangers are yet more obvious and startling. Without the rule changes of the early twentieth century, the game would likely have never grown much beyond the sandlot level. And indeed, before 1905 many colleges were considering dropping football altogether in favor of rugby. With the new rules and safeguards of the early twentieth century in place, however, football began to grow. Still, the game remained terribly rough, and its appeal continued to lie largely within the college and athletic club ranks.

Two

Early African Americans in Football

In the early years of organized American football, there was some presence of African Americans. This mirrored the slight degree to which African Americans had been permitted to enter the American college ranks in general. African American colleges began playing football at the same time the sport was growing in other American schools. Tiny Biddle University and Livingston College, both of North Carolina, were the first African American schools to play a game of football. That game took place on Thanksgiving Day, 1892. Biddle won by the score of 4–0. (Touchdowns were then worth four points.) By the middle of the 1890s, many African American schools had established football teams. In 1900 there were teams at Howard, Lincoln, Tuskegee, Atlanta, Morehouse, Fisk, Meharry, Talladega, Knoxville, West Virginia State, Kentucky State, Jackson, and Wilberforce.

From the 1890s up to World War I, a few predominantly white colleges permitted African Americans to play. The geographic distribution of these institutions reflected the relative levels of racial prejudice that dominated the nation in those years. The South, of course, had no integration—in football or anything else. The West had none either, due not only to prejudice but also to the relative paucity of available African American players in the region. It was in New England, in upstate New York, and in the Midwest that African American players began to appear on predominantly white teams.

In 1888 the Amherst College football team had the first African American player. His name was William H. Lewis. Lewis played at Amherst for four years. Moreover, he was elected the team's captain in 1891. William Tecumseh Sherman Jackson joined Lewis at Amherst in 1890 and 1891. This was the first integration of an American college football team. Still, no other African Americans played for

11

Amherst until 1908. In that year an African American named Edward Gray not only played, he starred, earning a selection to Walter Camp's Third Honor Team, the equivalent of today's All-Americans. A generation later, in the 1923–1925 seasons, Charlie Drew starred for Amherst in football, as well as in basketball and track, and he was elected captain of the track team. In that era, an African American athlete elected to such a position of athletic leadership at a predominantly white college was, of course, quite a rarity. Drew later became a famous physician. During World War II he perfected important new techniques in the storage of blood.

Harvard, a national football power in the 1890s, had one African American, William H. Lewis, who played center. This was the same William Lewis who had played for Amherst. He had graduated and gained admission to Harvard Law School. Law, Medical, and other sorts of graduate and professional students were then eligible for varsity sports, and there were no restrictions on the number of years that one could play. Lewis starred for the Crimson in 1892 and 1893 and was a true standout player. In 1892 and 1893, football pioneer Walter Camp named Lewis to his Honor Team. In 1900 Camp used the turn of the century to occasion a naming of an All-Time All-American football team, and he named Lewis as his center. Harvard also boasted two other African American players, Howard Lee, a star tackle in 1896, and Clarence Matthews, who played end in 1904.

Next door to Harvard, William Arthur Johnson integrated football at MIT in 1890. Tufts College, as it was then called, boasted an integrated team from 1914 to 1916, with two African American players, Edward Morrison and William Brown. Perhaps influenced by nearby Amherst, Williams College also allowed a few African Americans to dot their football roster. George Chadwell played end for three full seasons at Williams from 1897 to 1899, and Ernest Marshall played tackle in 1906 and 1907. At Dartmouth, Matthew Bullock starred at end in 1901, '02, and '03, as did Leslie Pollard in 1908. Pollard's younger brother, Frederick Douglas "Fritz" Pollard, would later star at Brown and be a key figure in the breaking of the color line in the early professional game.

In 1905 William Craighead was a standout player at tiny Massachusetts State College, along with William H. Williams. Craighead was elected the team captain. Gerald Lew and Benjamin Hubert also played for Massachusetts in the pre–World War I era. A college in Springfield, Massachusetts, first associated with the town's YMCA, now Springfield College, was always a school with a strong devotion to athletics. Springfield was also a leader in the opening of football, as well as other sports, to all races. Eight African American athletes played football for Springfield before World War I.

Outside New England, two schools in upstate New York broke "the color line" in the early years. At Syracuse in 1913, 1915, and 1916, Joseph Edward Trigg starred on the football team, as well as on the usually lily-white crew team. B.T. Harvey was a top player for Colgate in 1916. He later coached for many years at Morehouse College in Atlanta.[1]

Anywhere further to the South, the presence of African American athletes on anything but segregated teams was minimal. And when it occurred, the enterprising school ran risks. Western Pennsylvania's tiny Washington and Jefferson College, for example, was the only school in the state to achieve any integration in the early twentieth century (none, for example, at the University of Pittsburgh, the University of Pennsylvania, or Penn State). Washington and Jefferson College regularly slated some Virginia schools on its fall schedule. Invariably this led to problems. In 1923, Washington and Lee was visiting W and J, and the visitors discovered their host was planning to play a "colored boy." His name was Charles West. Back in Virginia, Washington and Lee learned of this and immediately balked. They phoned their coach, ordering him to issue an ultimatum—there would be no game unless Washington and Jefferson benched West. Washington and Jefferson refused to sit West down. Washington and Lee would not take the field. There was no game, and since then the two schools have not played one another.[2] Anywhere else in the South, the story would have been much the same, save, of course, for the greater likelihood of such an incident inciting violence as well as a boycott. Jim Crow was strictly enforced throughout the South, and in a violent endeavor like football, which obviously plays psychologically close to the edge of other forms of violence, the idea of mixing the races was unthinkable to all bigots and fellow travelers of the day.

In the Midwest a few schools broke ranks with the dominating segregationists. With its stern heritage of abolitionism and historic integration, Oberlin College in Ohio was one of the leaders. William Washington played for Oberlin from 1897 to 1899. Samuel Morrell played and lettered there in 1901 and 1902. Nathaniel Brown did the same in 1908 and 1909. Only a few other Midwestern schools dared to allow African Americans to play football. At the University of Illinois, Roy Young played and lettered in 1904 and 1905, as did Herbert H. Wheeler in 1906. The furor over their playing was considerable, and no African Americans again played for the Illini until Claude "Buddy" Young starred for them in the 1940s. By then, Illinois had erected barriers against African Americans playing any varsity sports. When Buddy Young appeared, his talents were so great that the school relented, though in a most peculiar way, as they forged a revised set of rules that forbade African Americans from participating in any varsity sports except football and track, where, not coincidentally, Young was, respectively, an All-American and the AAU 100- and 200-yard sprint champion, all the more impressive an achievement given that Young was only 5'4".[3]

Michigan State University, then a minor sports institution (it was not in the Big Ten Division until 1940), allowed one African American on its football team, Gideon Smith, who played there from 1913 to 1915. In the Big Ten, the University of Michigan played one African American, George Jeweth, in 1890. Thereafter, only the University of Minnesota and the University of Iowa allowed any integration before World War I. Minnesota had two African Americans playing for them from 1901 to 1904—Horace Bell and Bob Marshall. Iowa saw only one African American player, Albert A. Alexander, in 1910. The only other major Midwestern school that had any integration before World War I was the University of Nebraska. Back in 1892 and 1893, George Flippin played halfback. William N. Johnson and Robert Taylor each played for Nebraska from 1900 to 1904, and Clinton Ross was a standout tackle there in 1913.[4]

In these early years, beyond All-Americans William Lewis of Harvard and Edward Gray of Amherst, there were a few true standouts among the early African American players. One was Frederick Douglas "Fritz" Pollard. Pollard played for Brown in 1915 and 1916. He was really one of the prototype flashy scatback runners. Tacklers of the day had seen few like him, with his combination of darting moves, speed, and power. In 1916, almost singlehandedly, Pollard led an otherwise outmanned Brown team to decisive victories over such powers as Rutgers, Yale, and Harvard. Pollard made All-America that year, and his play led Brown to the Rose Bowl.[5]

The pre–World War I years thus saw a few cracks in the walls of racial segregation, but it was during the war years in the 1917 and 1918 seasons that the most visible and celebrated of early African American college football players truly caught some of the sports public's imagination. This was "the magnificent one," as he was called—Paul Leroy Robeson. While standouts like Lewis, Gray, and Pollard won the praise of football players, coaches, and commentators, the expressions of respect invariably raised the specter of race—"Pollard, the great Negro running back," etc. This revealed no limitation on Pollard's or anyone else's ability, but for reasons that involved a combination of athleticism and the elusive qualities of charisma, Robeson somehow transcended at least a little of this pigeonholing, if only in the minds of a few fans. Many reporters still focused on the issue of race. "Paul Robeson, the gigantic Negro back" was a refrain of several newspapermen who covered Rutgers football. Even here, though, the attitude was generally one of awe. Some simply called Robeson the greatest living football player. Whatever were the qualities that went into the transcendent characteristics of Robeson's talents on the football field, some may have stemmed from the fact that he was so multi-talented in all areas of his life that this supreme competence and confidence could resonate in many who witnessed him. Robeson was a most remarkable man. In his athletic achievements alone, in addition to being an All-American football player at Rutgers, Robeson lettered in three other sports. He was the star catcher on the baseball team; the dominant center on the basketball team, and a champion discus and javelin hurler in track and field. Beyond sports, Robeson was also the valedictorian of his Rutgers class. Additionally, Robeson's talents as a singer, actor, orator, debater, political activist and writer, which would make him so famous later on, were all in evidence in these years too, though the director of the university glee club rejected his audition. His "pitch" would make him "stick out," but not in the way Rutgers' choral director anticipated.[6]

With the World War I era, some schools, including Rutgers, found themselves playing some of their games against squads from various Army and Navy stations. A few of these teams had African Americans on their rosters, this shift being part of an overall series of adjustments that were occurring in the nation with the exigencies of war emergencies and production demands. In 1919 the still sizable U.S. Armed Forces held an internal Olympics, and African Americans competed there too. These shifts of behavior and outlook had occurred with wholesale movements of populations, with hastily planned industrial and housing situations that sometimes compromised older segregation traditions. It was not that any major government or individual figure was working for institutional integration at this time, although General John J. Pershing wanted it (which was why some derisively referred to him as "Black Jack"). It was simply that the war unleashed such a torrent of change that much slipped by that earlier customs of more leisurely times would have curtailed.

In many parts of the country, the shock of the sudden shift in demographics prompted some severe backlashes. African American hopes were rising amidst the wartime changes, but white recalcitrance was growing too. President Wilson's own racist sensibilities were well known—and largely accepted, as well as applauded. To the degree there had been any progress in the integration of Federal bureaucracies, Wilson put a stop to it. More broadly, the resonation felt by many Americans from D.W. Griffith's racist film *The Birth of a Nation*, which Griffith originally wanted to title *The Klansman*, gave fuller reification to many prejudices in the nation. Directly as a result of the film, the KKK was reborn, its original organization having died out in the 1890s, apparently believing it had accomplished its mission. With such clashings of hope and reaction, racial violence indeed tinged many cities during and immediately after the war years where whites and blacks had only recently mingled.

Some African Americans had hoped the geographic and job changes would lead to a better life. African American soldiers hoped their military service would enhance their social status. For many whites the shifts were regarded, at best, as a temporary inconvenience, and when any changes appeared to be of a more permanent nature, some white prejudices grew into overt anger and into desires to make sure no such changes would gain permanence. Questions about factory layoffs after the war increased tensions all around. Amidst such tensions, in 1917 and 1918 riots broke out in Philadelphia, Tulsa, Duluth, and Houston. In 1918 a particularly bad outburst of violence also occurred in East St. Louis, Illinois, where 49 people died (39 of whom were African American). In Chicago in the summer of 1919, the accidental drifting of a young African American swimmer in Lake Michigan onto a segregated white beach prompted hysterical whites to hurl stones at him. The swimmer was knocked unconscious and drowned. The already severe tensions in Chicago boiled over into a full week of riots, leaving 2000 homeless, 537 injured, and 38 dead, 23 of whom were African Americans. Elsewhere in the country that summer, an estimated 120 others died in incidents of racial violence.[7]

It was during the bitterly tinged years of wartime and post-war social adjustments that sports like football witnessed further changes in the racial composition of teams. Some moved forward, others backwards. Schools like Amherst, Tufts, Syracuse, Washington and Jefferson, Colgate, Iowa, Michigan State, and Oberlin brought new African American talent onto their football teams. Iowa's Frederick "Duke" Slater was most famous here, earning All America honors in 1919 and 1921. Meanwhile, other schools that had integrated before the war, like Illinois and Harvard, returned to all white customs. Most schools' teams continued to be strictly segregated too. Still, a few others opened the racial lines a bit in the decade after the war. Among them were the University of Vermont, Bates College, New York University, Columbia

University, Butler University of Indianapolis, Coe College of Iowa, and Northwestern University. NYU and Columbia had to contrive some clever tricks to disguise their integration when confronted with potential problems. Columbia once successfully mollified a group of recalcitrant officials at the still all-white United States Naval Academy with a claim that a certain dark skinned player was "Cuban." They may have picked up the tactic from nearby baseball manager John McGraw. McGraw was never successful with it, but the Columbia football team was. Further South, other schools were not so easily persuaded. The 1923 incident between Washington and Jefferson College and Washington and Lee was typical. Southern institutions were simply not going to change from within.

Out West, the University of California at Berkeley integrated when Brice Taylor made the team in 1928. California went to the Rose Bowl that year where they were slated to play Georgia Tech. The Georgians put up a huge fuss about playing against a black man. They demanded that Taylor be benched. Cal. stonewalled with the terse response: "the University of California team had been invited to play and ... Taylor was a member of the team." A few Georgia Tech players wanted to boycott the game, but the squad decided not to pass on the Rose Bowl. Taylor played, and he played well, although Georgia Tech prevailed 8–7. This was the famous "Wrong Way Riegels" game in which a player for Cal., Roy Riegels, picked up a fumble and ran 59 yards with it toward the wrong goal. A teammate (Benny Lom) stopped him on his own one-yard line, where the Georgia Tech team tackled him. From there, Berkeley tried to punt, with the exhausted Lom to do the punting. The punt was blocked for a safety, with the resulting two points being the margin of victory for the Southerners. The Berkeley players elected Riegels their captain the next year. The Atlanta papers, of course, went into great detail about Riegels' miscue. They printed not a word about Taylor.[8]

Three

The Emerging Pro Game

While the college game was going through hiccoughs of forward, backward, and sidestep movements in regard to the inclusion of African American athletes, the decade after World War I was also the time when sports entrepreneurs attempted to institute professional football at a serious level. There had been professional football in the early decades of the twentieth century, but it was at quite a small scale, and it left no lasting institutional structure.

In 1902 a few baseball men, notably the Philadelphia Athletics' Connie Mack and the Pittsburgh Pirate's Barney Dreyfuss, attempted to start fully professional football teams, organized in a league over significant stretches of geography. To try to capture fans, they used the same team names as their famous baseball clubs. Mack's and Dreyfuss's clubs were thus the Philadelphia Athletics and the Pittsburgh Pirates. Both owners hoped their football enterprises would make off-season money as well as offer some of their baseball players opportunities not only to make extra cash but to encourage them to stay in shape during the off season. With this in mind, Mack tried, for example, to employ the immensely talented but equally notoriously misbehaving George Edward "Rube" Waddell for his football Athletics. He also believed Waddell's name would bring out more crowds, as Waddell had almost singlehandedly pitched the A's to the pennant that summer and made the A's the toast of Philadelphia. With much the same sort of publicity in mind, Dreyfuss hired New York Giant pitcher Christy Mathewson for the football Pirates.

The 1902 season then marked the first time that professional football teams played from locales as far apart as Pittsburgh and Philadelphia. But this effort at the first sort of "national" league did not last beyond the one year it was attempted. The game was just too brutish and violent, so fan interest just was not going to grow. Mathewson's baseball manager, John McGraw, feared injury to his star pitcher, so

Dreyfuss never used Mathewson. Connie Mack was equally unfortunate with his baseball star. Rube Waddell proved even less susceptible to discipline in the context of football's mere one game a week regimen than he had been in baseball. Waddell never actually played. Some said he was afraid of the game's violence; others said he was too drunk. It may have been a combination of the two. Waddell and many other baseball players certainly found the nature of the early twentieth century gridiron game to be rather rough, though Waddell had played plenty of football back in his native Butler County, Pennsylvania. Baseball owners and managers came to the same conclusion and decided the risk of injury to baseball stars was too great. Baseball was the nation's only successful professional team game, and no one could see how any challenge could be mustered, or even why it should be attempted. Football was left to its own, largely localist, devices.

What marks early "professional football" left were quite narrow geographically. Western Pennsylvania had been a cradle for professional football going back to the 1890s, with various clubs in Pittsburgh and neighboring towns smashing one another every autumn weekend. The athletic clubs of Pittsburgh established football teams as far back as the 1880s. They grew quite competitive. The simple matter of city bragging rights motivated club managers to seek the best players. Victories in football games would stimulate club membership and permit a charging of higher dues. More importantly, club leaders regularly bet on their club's games, and they did anything they could to ensure their wagers. Towns began to pay various people to play for them, and many establishments, factories, and saloons gave football stars convenient forms of employment to keep them happy and content.

The brutish game also maintained a very strong life outside Pittsburgh in the small mill and coal towns in and around Western Pennsylvania. Nearby, the socio-economically similar mill towns of Eastern Ohio also proved fertile sites for the growth of the game at a professional level. What it was (and is) in the culture of this region that made it so conducive to the support of football can be the subject of rich, if ultimately inconclusive conjecture. The crude nature of the game mirrored the harsh life of the mines and mills that employed the mass of working men in the region. It also mirrored some of the harshness of the life in East Europe from which so many of the region's mill and mine workers had emigrated. Football also provided an outlet of semi-controlled violence for these men who labored under rugged conditions. While it is a generalization bordering on caricature, the physical size of so many of the East Europeans was also a useful trait for the game, especially in regard to its brutish style of play at the turn of the century. The plethora of small towns in the region and the strong identity citizens had to locale also stimulated strong fan support. Throughout the twentieth century, Pennsylvania and Ohio were the two states with the greatest number of communities with populations between 10,000 and 50,000. Unlike farm communities, there was sufficient proximity here to organize the number of lads needed for football games, and unlike the inner cities, there was sufficient space for the game to be played. The inner cities and the tiny town and farm communities in states like Indiana and Kentucky would produce basketball players. Pennsylvania and Ohio produced football players.

Whatever the other root causes, once football gained a toe hold in the region's culture, it grew and remains a most important part of the culture, with each generation of youth turning to the game as a virtual rite of passage. To this day, even though so many alternative pastime have since grown available, in every town in Western Pennsylvania and Eastern Ohio, every Friday autumn evening is devoted to local football. The religiosity of devotion here is approached by no other area of the nation, save perhaps some of the communities of Western Louisiana and Eastern Texas. The numbers of professional players that have come out of the 60-mile radius around Pittsburgh are legion. Among the quarterbacks alone, for example, the region produced Johnny Unitas, Joe Montana, Dan Marino, Johnny Lujak, George Blanda, Len Dawson, Joe Namath, Terry Hanratty, Bernie Kosar, Vinnie Testaverde, and Jim Kelly. (An old joke among football people, now outdated with the proliferation of telephone area codes, used to ask: How does a college coach find a quarterback? Answer: He picks up the phone and dials 412, the area code of Western Pennsylvania.) The number of great Western Pennsylvania linemen are even more numerous. In total, and yet even more in ratio to population, the region's contribution to the top college and professional football ranks is approached by no other part of the country. Baseball's greats have come from all over, with no particular geographic wellspring of talent. But the undeniable center of American football, particularly in its early days, was and remains the little region that starts on the western slope of the Allegheny mountains in Pennsylvania and rolls across the northern panhandle of West Virginia into the little mill towns of Eastern Ohio. That's football country.

While schools and colleges in Western Pennsylvania grew football crazy in the early twentieth century, communities in the region began to develop sports clubs. By the late nineteenth century, the city of Pittsburgh, like most major American industrial centers, was awash with athletic clubs. The most famous clubs in the city were the Allegheny Athletic Association and the Pittsburgh Athletic Club. But fire departments also had their own teams, as did such businesses as the Homestead Steel Works, Latrobe Steel, and the Edgar Thompson Works. Some "company towns" in the area, like McKees Rocks, Butler, Freeport, and Etna, had their own teams. And many other Western Pennsylvania towns formed squads too. Some felt that sports constituted a safe form of venting for the working classes. The sense of a society without a safety valve, a sense derived from the perception of a closed frontier, drew many to seek avenues for manly outlet, now that, metaphorically at least, there were no buffalo or Indians to be driven to the brink of extinction. Whatever the social and psychological factors, football and other sports teams spread throughout late nineteenth-century Western Pennsylvania.

While there was a straightforward desire in these new athletic clubs for simple health and exercise, that goal easily yielded to a desire to win at a particular sport. In most communities, the latter desire dominated. Here the ego-driven issue of bragging rights and the obvious desire to win the bets placed on football games entered the fray. In the summer, the clubs played and bet on baseball; in the autumn they bet on football. In the Pittsburgh area, the football leagues of these clubs quickly implanted themselves in the hearts and minds of local sports followers already predisposed to the game anyway.

The Pennsylvania athletic clubs played games against local colleges as well as against one another. The rivalries between these clubs was intense, and they began to seek athletes who could put them ahead of the others. It was here that they began to pay people to play. At first, game winners received prizes like jewelry and watches, which many of the players then pawned for cash. In November of 1892, Pittsburgh's Allegheny Athletic Association, one of the most prominent sports clubs in the city, was preparing for a big game against their arch rival, the Pittsburgh Athletic Club. They decided to recruit what came to be called a "ringer." His name was Pudge Heffelfinger. Heffelfinger had been a football star at Yale, the most successful college football team of the nineteenth century.* The Allegheny Athletic Association paid Heffelfinger $500 to play against the Pittsburgh Athletic Club. Allegheny won, and Heffelfinger became the first athlete actually to

---

*To illustrate Yale's former success in football, a classic trivia question asks: what school has produced the most All-American football players in the history of the game. The answer: Yale, as they produced dozens of stars in the game's early days. (Since 1920, Notre Dame has produced the most.)

be paid to play American football, thus the game's first professional. On Heffelfinger's recommendations, the Allegheny Association sought others who would play for pay. Other clubs howled about Allegheny's tactics, but there were no rules, as would come contemporaneously in the Olympic movement, and there were obviously no legal strictures governing such matters. Rival clubs had to join in the practice, lest they wanted to be laughed at as noble losers. Thus professional football was ignobly christened in Western Pennsylvania.

While athletic clubs laced their rosters with paid ringers (and colleges and universities began to play fast and loose with amateurism as well), it was a short step from there for associations to evolve from situations with a few professionals into clubs with mostly professionals, and finally into all-professional outfits. The money was not huge in those days, and all the "professionals" had to rely on other sources of income in their lives, but the idea of paying some players and not others could cause irritation, especially if some of the professionals, in contrast to a man like Heffelfinger, were not significantly better than many of their amateur teammates. Out in the town of Latrobe, some sixty miles east of Pittsburgh, team owners had a different idea. In 1895 they formed football's first all-professional team. Latrobe's management had to scrounge for sports clubs and colleges who would play them. They relied on gate receipts to gather the funds to pay the players. It worked, and the Latrobe club proved a going concern for a decade.[1] Others copied the pattern, and professionalism began to inch forward.

Four
Ohio Football

    While shifting from the norm of amateur clubs, to clubs with a sprinkling of professional "ringers," to fully paid teams, the game's next big step involved other clubs of the Latrobe variety proliferating to such a point that they could play good games against one another and attract sufficient popular followings to sell enough tickets to make the enterprise a financial success for almost everyone involved. Here the breakthrough came in the Western half of the football cradle—Eastern Ohio. Like Pittsburgh, the mill towns of late nineteenth-century Eastern Ohio were football crazy. By the early twentieth century, the professional/athletic club football circuit of Pittsburgh had begun to decline. Perhaps the fighting for the best players ultimately robbed club fans of a sense of identity with teams whose players had no links to the membership any more. Perhaps the sense of winning came to be seen purely in terms of who buys the best talent. The efforts by Connie Mack and Barney Dreyfuss to build a broader league, even though they failed, may have left the old system looking a trifle feeble in the eyes of many fans, particularly in comparison to professional baseball. The significance of town to town rivalries in Western Pennsylvania also muddied with the ever hovering presence of Pittsburgh, which could not sportingly compare with its little neighbors, nor apparently sustain a successful enterprise in competition with comparable cities like Philadelphia. In contrast, out in Ohio the town rivalries held a resonation among the football fanatics. In Akron, Youngstown, Zanesville, Steubenville, Canton, Lorain, Warren, and many other towns, athletic clubs proliferated. There was no one overbearingly large city in the mix, and the size of many of the burgeoning industrial towns yielded sufficient support and ticket purchases. In 1910, Akron's population, pushed by the growing automobile tire industries, had swelled to 69,000. Canton's reached 50,000. As in the Pittsburgh area, the town-town rivalries in eastern

Ohio were intense, and club managers began to seek the best talent they could buy.

The search for "ringers" involved the same story as had occurred in Western Pennsylvania. In this context, one of Ohio's clubs, the Shelby Athletic Club, hired a player in 1904 named Charles W. Follis, a great all-around athlete who happened to be African American. Follis thus became America's first black professional football player. Follis played in Ohio for two seasons. Two other African Americans played in Ohio during the first decade of professional football teams. One was Charles "Doc" Baker. He played for Akron from 1906 to 1908 and in 1911. The other was Clarence "Smoke" Fraim, who played for Toledo from 1914 to 1916. In various years between 1911 and 1920, a Hatian athlete named Henry McDonald played for a team in Rochester, N.Y., known as the Jeffersons. Another African American, Gideon Smith, played in one game for Canton, Ohio, in 1915 before going on to play for Michigan State.[1]

A key to the success of professional football in early twentieth-century Ohio was the rivalry between two of the towns, Massillon and Canton. The clashes (and wagers) between these two towns provided much of the needed heat for early fan interest. In 1903 the newly formed Massillon club (the "Tigers") defeated Canton in a rather bloody game. With hired professionals from Pittsburgh, they went on to defeat a team from Akron, the East Akron Athletic Association. Massillon's defeat of Akron prompted their managers to claim the "amateur" football title of Ohio. Because of the way they imported players, with the rest of the teams then following suit, Massillon's success started professional football in Ohio. Along with Massillon, Canton was most aggressive in the recruiting of paid players. Thus when the two towns met on the gridiron, everyone knew the game was "for keeps." The brutality of the games was enormous, and this apparently stimulated little fan revulsion; indeed, the early fans grew ever more passionate.

Ohio football's popularity grew among a wider circle of fans in 1906 when the rules of the game were changed and the frightful frequency of injuries and deaths declined. The Canton—Massillon game remained the game for fans in the region. Awareness grew of the quality of play and of the games' significance outside the region. Eastern sportswriter Grantland Rice wrote, "there have been a few football games before. Yale has faced Princeton, Harvard has tackled Penn, and Michigan and Chicago have met in one or two steamy affairs. But these were not the real product when measured by the football standard set by the warring factions of Stark County, Ohio, now posing the football limelight." Adding to the Ohio football fan's swagger, Rice added a bit of poetry:

> In days of old when Knights were bold,
> And barons held their sway—
> The atmosphere was fire, I hear,
> With "war" cried day by day.
> From morn to night, they'd scrap and fight
> With battle ax and mace—
> While seas of blood poured like a flood
> About the market place.
> But no fight ever fought beneath the shining sun
> Will be like that when Canton's team lines up
>   with Massillon.[2]

No sooner did the Massillon–Canton rivalry arise than it would grow so intense as to be self-destructive. In 1906 false rumors spread of gamblers and teams conspiring to fix games. This, along with a general overspending for talent by the team owners, would temporarily destroy professional football in Ohio.

Canton had recruited a very strong team for the fall of '06, and when Massillon surprisingly won the second of their two encounters with Canton, rumors flew that the Canton coach intentionally threw the game while in cahoots with gamblers. These allegations were printed in the Massillon newspaper, whose editor owned the Massillon team. The charges were never substantiated, but the story corroded everything. If people in Massillon, including the newspaper's editor, felt they were doing Canton in with their tactics, they did not realize how they were engaging in overkill. Fan interest suddenly waned, not just in Massillon but throughout Eastern Ohio. For the rest of the season, Canton and other clubs played before mere handfuls of spectators. Team revenues vanished. Players were not paid. Clubs folded. Professional football would not reappear in Ohio in any significant form until 1912.

When professional football reappeared, the fears of fixed games appeared to have subsided, but the game could do little more than limp along for three seasons. Then in 1915 came a shift of fortunes with the arrival of the professional game's first real star—Jim Thorpe. Thorpe, of course, had been a national hero when he won the decathlon at the 1912 Olympics, and the awe with which he was held among sports fans did not dim even though he had to relinquish his medals for having played semi-professional baseball a few summers before his Olympic triumph. (It has never been fully clear why sports officials made an example of Thorpe as they did. Many American Olympians had dabbled in summer baseball, though, unlike Thorpe, they usually played under assumed names. Racism may very well have been a factor in Thorpe being singled out. Some said Thorpe never fully recovered from the entire incident, especially because he had accepted the advice to admit his guilt in anticipation of a light wrist slap.) Despite the Olympic setback, Thorpe had also made a reasonable dent in the ranks of professional baseball, playing for John McGraw's New York Giants and with the Cincinnati Reds. Thorpe fielded and ran the bases superbly. He could get around on anyone's fastball, but he always had trouble hitting a curve. Thorpe proved somewhat a disappointment in baseball only because people fully expected he would be nothing less than the game's biggest star. While that did not happen in baseball, it certainly did occur in football.

With Thorpe's entry into the game of professional football in 1915, fan interest shot upward. Games which had usually drawn 1500 were now drawing 7000, and Thorpe did not disappoint. Thorpe was not only a great player, he was a great enforcer of discipline in the game. When the Haitian Henry McDonald and his Rochester teammates were playing Thorpe and Canton in 1917, McDonald was attacked by a racist player for Canton, a West Virginian named Earle "Greasy" Neale, who would later coach both Washington and Jefferson College to the Rose Bowl in 1922 and the Philadelphia Eagles to the NFL championship in 1948 and 1949. Neale yelled at McDonald, "Where I come from black is black and white is white, and they never mix!"[3] Thorpe stepped into the fray, and Neale backed down. McDonald said that was the only racist incident he faced. Follis and Baker had faced much worse, with many cheap shots that could have caused career threatening injuries. For all three there was a constant bombardment of taunts and racial slurs. For McDonald at least, Thorpe's word was the law on the field.[4]

Even with the enforcement efforts of a man like Thorpe, the few African Americans in early professional football had to endure enormous hardships. They had to accept as well-meaning such nicknames as "jig," "dinge," and "burr-head." The "N" word was incessant. They were expected to "know their place" when it came to yielding a space on the bench or better locker space to white teammates. Many whites refused to allow black teammates to drink from the same water bucket or use any of the team's locker or shower facilities. And when teams traveled, it was a fact of life that "colored players" were going to have to find "colored lodgings" on their own.[5]

By keeping the focus on the true game, rather than on the likes of Greasy Neale, and by drawing thousands of fans to the stadiums, Thorpe singlehandedly made the professional game flourish. Then World War I came and temporarily cut football's strength. Countless players went off to the armed forces. One sidelight here did temporarily discombobulate the traditional power relations of the game. This came with the establishment of the Great Lakes Naval Training Station outside Chicago. The commanders there decided to field a team. They had so many top college players that they were unbeatable, and in January 1919 they actually played in the Rose Bowl, and won. The Great Lakes' success further fueled interest in the idea of post-college men playing a respectable game, and fan interest near the Great Lakes Station grew in Illinois and Wisconsin, where college football was already popular, to accompany the rabid fans of Ohio and Pennsylvania. With the war ending, Thorpe and the pro game were back in 1919. And now significant fan interest had spread to new areas of the nation.

Five

New League,
New Opportunities

In 1919 a group of football people thought they could make a go of organized professional football on a wider geographic level, pulling together, they hoped, the fan interest in the East, the Midwest, and, of course, in Pennsylvania, West Virginia, and Ohio. Together these entrepreneurial men formed what was first called the American Professional Football Association, which two years later they renamed the National Football League. The NFL of that era had little about it that was comparable to the modern operation of professional football. It was quite a rag-tag outfit. Fan attendance was meager. Pay was tawdry, in some cases non-existent.

In baseball the sufficient fan interest, organizational maturity, and ensconced racism was such that African Americans would continue to find themselves excluded. Simultaneously, paralleling the renaissance of African American culture in the era, enterprising African Americans, led by Arnold "Rube" Foster, expanded the Negro Baseball Leagues. Pro football at this time was simply too primitive for such "sophisticated," "separate but equal" structuring. It was hardly clear that any pro football league would survive, much less one that was all black or all white. The idea of segregation, or any other sort of segmenting, could not be considered, no matter how some owners may have wished to do so. Even if there had been any such rules or customs, any team owner in the league could have easily broken them with nothing to fear from the other teams, as everyone knew that any fines or other discipline imposed with the underlying threat of a boycott could kill off the livelihoods of everyone in the league. It was not that owners of early professional football teams wanted African American athletes to play, they simply could not do much to stop anyone else from employing them.

In this primitive spirit of begrudging ambivalence about the race question, one football club in Akron, Ohio, known as "the Pros," signed Brown University star Fritz Pollard. A few other African Americans followed Pollard into the early professional ranks. Between 1920 and 1933, thirteen African Americans played in the NFL. For Pollard and various African Americans, the road in the early NFL was a rugged one indeed. In every game came the taunts and cheap shots. It took a special style and strength of character to survive in such a world, one in which violence was a fact of life and where the fine line from normal game violence to racially motivated attacks was being constantly crossed. Pollard knew how to handle the taunts, and in most ways he triumphed. Over and over, Pollard would hear opposing players yelling "let's get him." No one offered any sympathy, and he was hit high and low. But every time, Pollard just got back up and played harder. And every time he heard such words as "You little black...," Pollard said, "I'd look at 'em and grin." Pollard also made a habit, whenever he was knocked down, of rolling over on his back and thrusting his cleats straight up. Otherwise he knew he was going to be hit even though the referee's whistle had blown.[1]

Back in the early twentieth century, Charles Follis apparently had the same self-confidence and inner serenity. He dealt with the taunts without ever retaliating. Such strength of character has never been required, to the same degree, of Anglo and other non-minority sports figures. Indeed, some "majority" athletes have made themselves more famous by being tempestuous. Rarely has an angry temperament hurt the career of a white athlete, especially in football, as it has a minority player. A few whites, like early 1960s football player Joe Don Looney and baseball player John Rocker in 1999–2000, have let their tempestuous natures get the better of them. For minorities, far less belligerence tends to yield far more punishment. This was ever more the case back in the era of Jim Crow and extreme racial prejudice. The added demands on minorities' temperaments have been ever present. Those who had the athletic ability but not such a temperament tended to fail. This added burden has been particularly difficult in football, where the demand for serenity of spirit comes in an endeavor that is so violent. (When it comes in a sport like boxing, the duality of serenity and violence can prove virtually schizophrenic.)

Follis' example of temperament was apparent to observers at the time, and would have an impact later on as well. When Follis played baseball for the College of Wooster in Ohio in 1901 and 1902, he also encountered endless physical and verbal abuse. But he never retaliated with words or violence. A contemporary of Follis, Branch Rickey, played for nearby Ohio Wesleyan, and he witnessed Follis' play. Rickey was impressed with Follis' athletic ability; even more, he noted Follis' temperament. Years later, when Rickey recruited Jackie Robinson to break the color line in baseball, it was the example of Follis that Rickey raised to instruct Robinson as to the necessity of never retaliating to the inevitable taunts, attacks, and harassments.[2]

Because of both talent and strength of temperament, Fritz Pollard did more than merely survive his hate-laced violent world of 1920s professional football. He excelled. In Akron he became the team leader. In those days, coaches' roles were more limited. Plays had to be called on the field. Indeed, substitutes (then a rarity other than for an injury) were theoretically not allowed to talk to the quarterback upon entering the game, though, of course, they often did. Pollard was the field leader of the Akron Pros, usually calling the entire game. He gained the respect of the team, both with his ability and with his knowledge and savvy of the game. Consequently, from 1919 to 1921 Pollard was the real coach of the Akron Pros.[3]

Even while coaching at Akron, Pollard could not dress for games with the rest of the team. The Pros' owner, Frank Neid, owned a cigar factory, and Pollard changed for all games at the factory. He also could not eat at Akron restaurants or stay in any of the city's (or most of the road cities') hotels. Many Southerners had moved to the Akron area during the war for the jobs that were growing in the rubber industry. Their presence combined with the existing prejudice among the city's working and elite classes to make a fearsome set of sensibilities that was then impossible to surmount. In view of such a political state of affairs, Pollard's successes in Akron are all the more remarkable. In 1921 Pollard and the Akron Pros went undefeated (8–0–3).

Due in some measure to Pollard's influence, a few other African Americans were recruited to play in the early NFL. Pollard induced one of his best friends from his college days, Paul Robeson, to play for Akron in 1920 and 1921. Robeson's presence made the Pros an even more outstanding team. The Rutgers star was fearsome, both as a defensive tackle and as an offensive end. He was so big that no one could easily stop his acrobatic catches on offense, and his strength was such that he was extremely formidable on defense. Had Robeson been more fully committed to an athletic career, he could have readily become one of, if not *the* most outstanding football player of his era. But Robeson, a man of so many gifts, had other interests. Pollard's biographer asserts that Pollard actually got Robeson going on his musical career by introducing him to a woman, Florence Mills, who made it possible for Robeson to sing at the Winter Garden Theater in

Frederick Douglas "Fritz" Pollard. A star running back with Brown, Pollard played for an NFL club in Akron in the 1920s before team owners were able to coordinate an effective ban on African-American players. Pollard was not only a star player in the NFL, he also coached.

New York.[4] But Robeson was already deeply involved in music and theater. Meanwhile, Robeson was also enrolled at Columbia University Law School. How Robeson did all this—sing, act, go to law school, and play pro football—is a staggering thought. But he did it. He would go to classes during the week days, sing and act at various theaters in the evenings, hop the train from New York to Akron every Friday (presumably studying en route), practice with the team on Saturday, play on Sunday, head back to New York on Sunday night, and be back in class on Monday morning! Robeson's most distinguished biographer, Martin Duberman, does note that, amidst such a dizzying array of activities, Robeson's law school performance did not come close to matching the valedictorian stature he had attained as an undergraduate at Rutgers. He was a C/C+ law student, middle of his class, and his heart was not fully in it. Given all that was "on his plate," how could it? Neither football nor even the law would prove Robeson's true calling. Music and theater would capture his spirit. Even more, of course, Robeson became a dedicated political activist on behalf of African Americans and of the downtrodden everywhere. Though pro football was but a side bar in his fantastic life, Robeson never lost touch with Fritz Pollard, however, and they remained friends thereafter. Pollard served, indeed, as Robeson's personal manager for much of his music and theatrical career.[5]

Pollard left Akron after the 1921 season and then took part in organizing, coaching, and playing for a new team in Milwaukee, Wisconsin, called the Badgers. Robeson joined Pollard in Milwaukee for some of the 1922 season. Pollard also recruited another African American star from the college ranks, Iowa's Frederick "Duke" Slater. Meanwhile, other teams in the league also tapped some African American talent. A team in Hammond, Indiana, signed John Shelbourne, who had played at Dartmouth, and Jay Mayo Williams, who was given the not-so-playful nickname of "Inky." Williams had been Pollard's roommate at Brown.

Robeson never played football after 1922, and Shelbourne quit after that year too. But several other African Americans entered the league from 1923 to 1925. While African American representation was not huge, it was certainly better than either the total segregation of baseball or the huge barriers that boxers and other African-American athletes encountered. Still, the road was immensely difficult for these football players. When Canton visited New York for a game in 1926, for example, the New York team refused to play because one Canton player, Sol Butler, was black. The New York team owners supported the players, claiming the crowd would also object to Butler. Butler resolved the impasse by agreeing not to play.[6] In addition to such incidents, after the 1926 season, various business dynamics in professional football compelled the league to shrink in size, and with the reduction, the precious visibility of the little African American professional football talent began to diminish.

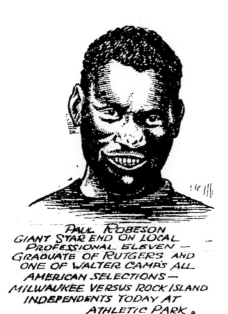

PAUL ROBESON
GIANT STAR END ON LOCAL
PROFESSIONAL ELEVEN —
GRADUATE OF RUTGERS AND
ONE OF WALTER CAMP'S ALL
AMERICAN SELECTIONS —
MILWAUKEE VERSUS ROCK ISLAND
INDEPENDENTS TODAY AT
ATHLETIC PARK.

Paul Robeson. While later famous for his singing, his theater and cinema performing, and his political activism, Robeson was also an All-American football player at Rutgers and played briefly in the NFL. He had a most fearsome presence on the field, so much so that journalists sought to caricature him in their drawings in ways which emphasized racial stereotypes, as was done here in a Wisconsin paper a few days prior to a game Robeson was to play in Milwaukee. (*Milwaukee Sentinel*)

The famous Harold "Red" Grange completed a highly publicized career at the University of Illinois in 1925. In a decade of larger than life sports heroes like Babe Ruth, Bobby Jones, Man 'O War, Bill Tilden, and Johnny Weismuller, Grange was football's answer. When Grange announced after the end of the '25 college season that he was ready to turn professional, NFL leaders were naturally eager to have him. Grange began playing professionally for the Chicago Bears in the late part of the 1925 season, and after the season was over he and a team of professional players traveled about the country playing exhibitions. The barnstorming tour was a smashing financial success, so much so that Grange felt he could make significant demands upon the Bears' owner, the always parsimonious George Halas. Grange's demands were certainly considerable. He wanted one-third ownership of the team. Halas refused him. Grange then sought to start his own team in New York. But with one NFL team already there, NFL owners immediately disapproved of the idea. The adventurous Grange then up and left the NFL altogether and attempted to start his own league, calling it the "American Football League." Grange was a great talent, with an ego to match. But his presence, enthusiasm, and playing were not enough to draw fans to cities all over the Northeast and Midwest, where the new AFL established clubs—New York, Brooklyn, Newark, Boston, Philadelphia, Cleveland, Rock Island, Illinois, and Los Angeles. This AFL failed in its first year; and when the league collapsed, surviving teams in the NFL embarked upon a somewhat sober consolidation.

With fewer players and fewer teams, the number of African Americans in the NFL then dwindled. Between 1926 and 1927 the number of teams in the NFL shrunk from 31 to 12. Pollard retired after 1926. By 1927 Duke Slater was the only African American left in the league. A few black players dotted rosters in the late '20s, but Slater was the only African American player of note.

Slater retired in 1931. This, of course, was the time that the Great Depression was at its worst. Teams were folding, and those that survived were constantly on the edge of bankruptcy. Rosters were trimmed and salaries cut. As in industries all over the nation, the specter of maintaining black employees while laying off whites did not sit well with some white owners, especially in businesses like football, where owners were concerned with fan appeal among the working classes. In the early 1930s the status of African Americans in the professional game appeared to be hanging by a thread.

Beyond the newness of the enterprise known as the National Football League, the image of the game continued to be problematic in regards to the hopes for any growth of popularity. In the post–World War I era, many Americans still maintained a bit of revulsion in regard to football. What was a virtue in the mill towns of Western Pennsylvania and Eastern Ohio, and among the working classes of Hammond, Indiana, South Chicago, Green Bay, Wisconsin, and Detroit, was not always fully appealing to the majority of the American middle class. What has been said about lacrosse—a game for thugs played by gentlemen—embodied the acceptance of *college* football in the public mind, that this was a slightly violent phase of male life, constituting a kind of last gasp of adolescence in which, much like fraternity pranks, college men should, within limits, be indulged before they grew up. Baseball players somehow enjoyed a contrasting image of eternal youth and innocence. And the traditional non-linkage of professional baseball to the college ranks was part of this sensibility. A typical baseball player was never considered in the class of a football player who had attended college. Football fans could rejoice in such rites of masculine passage through the college game, as well as getting out once a week every autumn and rooting for "their boys."

Professional football, in contrast, represented a far less innocent form of revelry and more sinister type of thuggery. The memories of all those crippling injuries and deaths in the early twentieth century, and the specter of huge men simply ramming each other and piling into scrums, held no aura of romance. Football in this era still played the classic five(or less)-yards-and-a-cloud-of-dust game. The fan-base growth in the 1920s came when the game boasted a rare exception to the boorish grunting style of the era. This came, for example, with the dazzling play of Red Grange (and many of his most spectacular, well-attended games occurred when he was playing college ball). Generally from 1919 to 1933, the professional game's appeal remained quite limited. There was some romance in the idea of invulnerable college lads taking a break from study and having a gentlemanly go at one another on a sporting Saturday afternoon, but the popularity of the game did not grow much beyond that imagery.

The style of the early game was not conducive to mass popularity. Kicking was actually the key to the game as it was played in those days (hence the game's name). When a team scored, the rules then allowed the opposition to choose whether then to kick or receive, and many chose the former. The key was to jockey for position by trading punts in order to pin the opposition back and hope for a fumble or a mistake. Long runs, passes, and sustained drives of over 30 yards were exceedingly rare. Brutish defense, strong kicking, and pouncing on the good break when it came—these were the essential ingredients to the game of that era. As a result, early football could simply be boring. Little offense was there to dazzle, and the oafish nature of defensive struggles had little of the tension and excitement of a pitchers' duel in baseball.

Professional football was also handicapped by a quandary over when to play. College football had a lock on Saturdays. (This was so much the accepted norm that the common term for second-guessing in those days was "Sunday Morning Quarterbacking.") Lighting questions and cold weather made night games difficult to impossible. Weekdays ruled out the attendance of many working class folks, who were the backbone of fan support in the pro game's early days. The big barrier was that Sundays were still taboo in the minds of many in a nation still replete with intensely religious communities. Through the decade of the 1920s, various cities, especially in the East, maintained laws which prohibited sports, including baseball, to be played on Sundays. Midwestern cities were more open on this point, but fans were still reticent, given the continued significance of the Sabbath for many. Football, therefore, had not much of a market to exploit. Considering all the obstacles, the game's owners and players of the 1920s fared remarkably well, but they never fared well enough to turn their enterprise into a major sports operation that could come within a shadow of the major sports of the nation—boxing, horse racing, and baseball.

With meager fan interest, professional football teams were financially poor and minimally organized. Teams set their own schedules; some played as few as half the number of games of others. There was no real league administration. (While still playing, Jim Thorpe was nominally the league's chief administrator in 1920.) Pro teams played non-league teams as often as they played their league brethren. In the '20s, NFL franchises involved such major, minor, and utterly obscure towns as Akron, Decatur, Rock Island, Dayton, Canton, Muncie, Hammond, Columbus, Evansville, Tonawanda, Racine, Marion (Ohio), Duluth, Frankford, Kenosha, and Pottsville,

Who won? What were the statistics? What were the records of the teams? Some of this vital information was actually unknown to the NFL in the 1920s. At off-season meetings, some debates broke out among team owners as to who actually won particular games or even who won the league championship in the prior season. After the 1925 season, for example, both Chicago (the Cardinals) and Pottsville, Pa., claimed the championship. Pottsville had the superior record, but Chicago contested the legitimacy of several of Pottsville's games. Pottsville had employed some of the famous former four Horsemen of Notre Dame, who had been banned by the league because of contract jumping. Harry Stuhldreher, for example, had signed with the NFL's Providence, Rhode Island, Steam Rollers, but while under contract had jumped to a non-league pro team in Hartford, Connecticut. Pottsville also played a game in Philadelphia, which the league had designated as the home territory of the Frankford Yellow Jackets. The Chicago (at first Racine, Wisconsin) Cardinals claimed that several of Pottsville's games should be disallowed and, then, that they were the rightful champions. The question was never fully resolved. Such controversies were inevitable in the rag-tag operations that were normal in the infant days of the NFL.

Attendance at pro games also had to compete with the more popular college game. As a result, some sizable cities in the region with big populations of football fans, notably Columbus and Pittsburgh, could not support a professional team very well. In the '20s both Columbus and Pittsburgh were home to the fabulously successful college teams of Ohio State, the University of Pittsburgh, and Carnegie Tech (now Carnegie Mellon University). In Pittsburgh the success of Pitt. and Carnegie Tech had helped chase out the old athletic clubs, and fledgling little professional football organizations were certainly no match for such big-time colleges. To avoid competition with colleges, some owners did attempt to have games on Sunday, but this did not work well, and with blues laws like those in the state of Pennsylvania, it often could not. (The city of Philadelphia would not allow any Sunday sports playing, including baseball, until 1933.)

Fan interest in early professional football was largely regional in character, more like lacrosse and ice hockey. In 1922 pro football had about as much coverage in Seattle as ice hockey had in Houston. It was within such a rag-tag context that some African Americans made inroads into the pro game, much like the African American baseball players who made it into the professional baseball ranks in the 1880s. The game had not sufficient national significance to raise enough hackles to engender the perceived need for segregation, and any such rules could not be enforced anyway.

The life of the African American pioneers in the fledgling NFL was rugged, more rugged indeed than the life of the average white player, who himself labored in obscurity compared with his counterparts in sports like baseball, boxing, and golf. Still, most of the 11 African Americans who played professionally in the 1920s did gain something. John Shelbourne and Paul Robeson played for a limited time and went on to other things (for Shelbourne it was teaching). Others of less athletic distinction had short careers, as did most whites, and the African American stars like Duke Slater and Fritz Pollard did stay in the league for a length of time and win a certain, albeit often begrudging, respect and fame.

While one certainly cannot candy coat the physical and verbal abuse all these pioneers experienced, the fate of the two African Americans who played in the NFL in the early 1930s—Ray Kemp and Joe Lillard—was even worse. Each would be on the receiving end of the same taunts, slurs, and "extra-curricular's." Each would also be hit by a series of ridiculously unfair events which led them to be tossed out of the professional game when an unwritten, though explicit, color barrier came down in the league in 1933.

Six

The Curtain Falls

Joe Lillard was a sensational athlete. He played professional basketball. In baseball he played in the Negro Leagues and was a great switch hitter for both power and average. His fielding was superb, and he showed great speed and cunning on the base paths. In football he could do everything—block fiercely, tackle hard; he was also one of the game's best punters and kickers (and in those days this included the important art of drop kicking*). As a running back he excelled, with both speed and power, and he could throw the ball both far and accurately. He could do it all.

An Iowa native, Lillard was going to play for the University of Minnesota in 1930. That summer, however, Minnesota's coach, Clarence "Doc" Spears, accepted an offer from the University of Oregon. Spears persuaded Lillard to go west with him. At Oregon that fall, Lillard was a standout on the freshman team, and in the following season he emerged as the team's star player. Oregon newspapers were all agog at the prospect of the usually lowly Oregon "Ducks" contending for West Coast football supremacy with the likes of such perennial powers as Stanford, Berkeley, and the University of Southern California. Salem's *Oregon Statesman* called Lillard "The main cog in the Webfoot Machine." Often referring to him as "Oregon's great colored halfback," *The Statesman* nicknamed Lillard "the Midnight Express." Elsewhere they called him "Shufflin' Joe." There was obviously more than a tinge of racism in the nicknames (and, more blatantly, Portland's *Oregon Journal* printed a condescending description of Lillard as "a not quite coal-black Negro boy"). Still, there were

---

Drop kicking was the means of converting field goals and points after touchdowns. It was a more unpredictable art, and someone who was good at it, like Lillard, was most valuable to his team. In high school he kicked a field goal of over 50 yards.

elements of joy and respect in the way the Oregon fans took to Lillard. His quality was undeniable, and he was singlehandedly pulling Oregon out of also-ran status into contention for a Pacific Coast Conference crown. Simply put, Lillard brought Rose Bowl fever to Oregon.[1]

On October 3, 1931, Lillard led Oregon in its season opener to a 9–0 shutout of the University of Idaho. He scored all the team's points. *The Oregon Statesman* reported that Lillard's runs had brought spectators to their feet. With the shutout, other sports reporters on the West Coast began to take note, and fans of rival schools grew a little nervous. The *Los Angeles Times* wrote pointedly of the new "Negro Star of the Oregon backfield."[2] While the victory over Idaho unsettled some, Idaho was hardly a power. Neighboring University of Washington, however, was picked to contend with USC and Stanford for the Pacific Conference crown that fall (hence a Rose Bowl bid). Washington was Oregon's next opponent. Oregon surprised the pundits and the press, winning the game by another shutout, 13–0. Again Lillard was the star of the game, intercepting two passes and scoring a touchdown. This sound defeat of Washington was a genuine upset, and West Coast football people now took very careful note of the new power in their midst.

Oregon's next game, on October 20, was to be against the University of Southern California. Such matters as the conference championship and the Rose Bowl bid were now very much in the offing. Before the season, USC people felt the Oregon game would be a breeze. Now they knew they had to prepare in earnest. That week the USC coaches went so far as to insert a black reserve player named Slick Stooks to play the role of Lillard during practices to "help" the team prepare to face Oregon's new star by practicing the spotting of someone who looked like Lillard. The race issue was certainly part of the picture in the minds of USC coaches.[3] Oregon, bluntly declared the partisan *Los Angeles Times*, stands "before the Trojans' path to the title."[4]

As the USC game approached, clouds began to form over Lillard. In the week prior to the October 13 game against Washington, the Oregon papers had announced that Lillard was under investigation for having played semi-professional baseball the previous summer for the Gilkerson (North Dakota) Union Giants, a "Colored" baseball team. Lillard admitted he had played but contended that he only received money as payment for driving one of the team's vehicles when they traveled.[5] The *Los Angeles Times* reported that Jonathan Butler, the then newly appointed commissioner of the Pacific Coast Conference, was questioning Lillard's eligibility.[6] Butler had been hired, in part, to investigate and resolve the question of amateurism among West Coast collegiate athletes. The *Los Angeles Times,* hardly fans of Oregon, noted that Butler, "who is new to the conference, seemed unaware that while semi-pro baseball is not permitted in his former conference, the Big 10, for years it has been overlooked in the Northwest under a gentlemen's agreement between the colleges." The *L.A. Times* knew that any strict enforcement of the rule about college football players playing summer baseball for pay would mark the decimation of many Pacific teams, including their hometown favorite USC.

On October 8 Butler declared Lillard ineligible. The University of Oregon's faculty athletic committee first went along with Butler's decision.[7] The next day, however, the Oregon committee voted to reinstate their star player. Meanwhile, Professor H.C. Howe, the University of Oregon's representative to the Pacific Coast Conference, was trying to lobby fellow members on behalf of Lillard. Upon their move to reinstate Lillard, the Oregon faculty announced that they had investigated and were "unable to find anything" to justify a suspension. The money Lillard earned that summer, they acknowledged, was for chauffeuring, not for playing baseball. The University of Washington officials did not take issue with the Oregon faculty's decision, and here the *Los Angeles Times* frankly noted, "were [Lillard] made ineligible, the ruling would hit at least a dozen players of other conference teams, several of whom are stars."[8]

With the University of Washington representative to the Pacific Coast Conference not objecting, Howe was able to convince his colleagues to vote a stay on Butler's ruling. Lillard then played and was instrumental in the defeat of Washington. The matter could have ended there, but P.C.C. Commissioner Butler would not drop it. Oregon's coach, "Doc" Spears, perhaps in a fit of anger over Butler's efforts, and perhaps believing that the matter was behind him, spouted off to the *Oregon Daily Journal.* He referred to Butler as "the 'Judge Landis' of coast football." Kennesaw Mountain Landis, of course, had become the tsar of major league baseball and ruled the game with a harsh, dramatic tone that was outwardly devoted to keeping the game clean (and lily white), and otherwise devoted to boosting his own insatiable ego. Butler had just come to the West Coast, and indeed appeared fully desirous of letting everyone know that he was in charge. The Lillard question was thus a matter upon which he was not going to relent. The fact that Oregon and Washington people appeared to bypass his judgment in regard to Lillard's eligibility combined with "Doc" Spears' harsh comments to raise his ire. Spears went further with the press, rhetorically asking why Butler does not make a full and careful study of such issues as semi-pro baseball playing throughout the conference. Spears had a point, as Butler was hired to do just that, but here he was seeking to make a splash with a decision based on minimal investigation in regard only to one player. "There are many players in the conference," opined Spears, "who have played semi-pro ball. Why doesn't [Butler] wait until he has the information on the whole bunch and throw them out together." Instead, complained Spears, Butler "comes to Oregon [and] singles out Lillard."[9]

With the defeat of Washington, with USC next in line, with a conference championship and Rose Bowl bid potentially at stake, Butler continued to press the issue. Meanwhile, The *Oregon Daily Journal* echoed many of Coach Spears' sentiments. Semi-pro baseball, they noted, "has always been a 'bugbear' to college football." But, they asked, "what about the baseball playing of Orve Mohler," USC's quarterback, and what about the "S.C. players [used] as extras in Hollywood feature films?" Why, the paper asked, could Butler not investigate all matters carefully, as he was hired to do? "Right off, [Butler instead] calls a special meeting" strictly in regard to Lillard. Pointedly, the *Daily Journal* lamented in a kind of final appeal, "It takes a dash of color to fill stadiums in these days of depression."[10]

At this critical juncture and under this sort of pressure, Butler likely figured his credibility and political clout had either to grow or die. On the day before the Oregon-USC game Butler offered his resignation to the P.C.C. board. They refused to accept it, and Butler then declared Lillard ineligible. He added a new charge here from the previous week's efforts—that Lillard had played a baseball game that summer up in Jamestown, North Dakota, and accepted money under the assumed name of "Johnson." This gave the other P.C.C. members the excuse of a new pretext, and with this Butler ended the gentleman's agreement about summer baseball playing by Pacific Conference football players. Doc Spears lamented, "I feel pretty sick about the development, but I guess there is nothing I can do about it." The University of Oregon's President, Arnold Bennett, also said he was surprised but offered no further comment. The next day, without Lillard, a completely dispirited Oregon team was trounced by USC 53–0. Oregon's season ended miserably. USC won the Pacific crown and went to the Rose Bowl.

Lillard was pilloried amidst some political crossfires, with the primary shots coming from an outsider who had come to the West Coast interested in establishing a reputation for himself as a take-charge man. Lillard's race made him an easy target for such a ploy, as did the fact that Oregon was "out of the loop" among the mainstays of West Coast collegiate sports. Had Lillard played for USC, like the latter's quarterback of the day, the matter would likely have never arisen. Somewhat like Jim Thorpe in regard to his Olympic medals, Lillard had gone along with the investigation, admitting his error. He knew full well that many other athletes had bent the rules in the summer exactly as he had. Like Thorpe, he probably expected a warning or some other mere wrist slap. Instead he found himself tossed permanently out of the P.C.C. Perhaps at the point of his dismissal he could have hired a lawyer and sued, but that was anything but normal in those days. Additionally, he probably could not have found representation; and even if he had found anyone, he would not have been able to afford it anyway. He had no choice but to swallow a most bitter pill. The cruel fates were not yet through with Lillard, however. They were just beginning to conspire against him.

Lillard left school and secured employment that fall with some touring professional football squads on the West Coast. With the NFL exclusively in the East and Midwest, such exhibitions were popular out West. In early December the tour was over, and Lillard moved back to the Midwest, settling in Chicago where he played in some more professional exhibitions in football and basketball. (Lillard had played for a Chicago team called the Savoy Big Five. Sponsored by the city's Savoy Ballroom, the team had been formed by a young sports entrepreneur named Abe Saperstein, and Lillard was one of the original players. This was the team later to become known as the Harlem Globetrotters.)

The quality of Lillard's play in exhibition football was such that, prior to the following season, he was invited to try out for the NFL's Chicago Cardinals. He made the team easily. The Cardinals were a weak NFL team. Even among Chicago's fans, the Cardinals were regarded as the city's second team, paling in attendance (and perceived to pale in quality) before George Halas' popular Bears. In some ways it was a similar contrast of sensibility that Chicago's baseball fans showed in regard to the Cubs and the White Sox. The Cubs and the Bears were the teams of the North Side. The Sox and the Cards played for the poorer Southsiders. The two baseball teams played in different leagues, however, so fans could accommodate both. In football, with a smaller fan pool to begin with, the Bears and Cards were in the same little league, so the city's football fans felt compelled to make more of a choice. The Bears were clearly the city's team; the Cards played to more meager crowds and received thinner coverage in the local press. In two of the city's larger papers, the *Tribune* and the *Herald and*

Examiner, coverage of the Bears was always deeper. The *Chicago Daily News* barely touched the Cardinals, aside from listing its game statistics and scores. This would be the Cards' unchanging fate until they finally relocated to St. Louis in 1960, later, of course, moving to Arizona where they have since resided.

Simple logic dictated that, aside from relocating, the one way out of second-fiddle status for the Cardinals was to develop a good team. The recruiting of a talented player like Joe Lillard thus made good sense, and in the early games of the 1932 season, Lillard certainly made an impact. He played well in a 19–0 defeat of a non-league team from Battle Creek, Michigan. In the first league game, a 7–7 tie with Portsmouth, Lillard ran well and drop kicked the all important extra point which tied the game. In the next week against the up-town rival Bears (NFL champions that year), the Cardinals again secured a tie, this time 0–0. Against the Bears, Lillard's play was crucial. He led the Cardinals, and the Bears, in rushing and was apparently the only highlight of the game on either side. Among his achievements was a fifty yard punt that pulled the Cardinals out of a tight spot on their own one-yard line. The *Chicago Herald and Examiner* sniffed, somewhat obnoxiously, about a game between "rival Chicago post-graduate teams," a signal of how college ball was still jauntily held as the preeminent form of football in the minds of many fans:

> The game, like the weather [it was a steady, cold drizzle], was fearful to behold. The only bright spot of the pastime being a dark one, Joe Lillard, a lanky Negro athlete....
> Lillard refused to be annoyed by the weather, and most of the entertainment, if indeed the spectacle of twenty-two tired businessmen going through the motions, very slow ones at that, of playing a football game can be called that, was provided by him.
> [Lillard made] the assembled addicts forget all about "Red" Grange and [Chicago's star fullback] "Bronko" Nagurski. Lillard, not Grange, provided what little opportunity there was to enthuse.... His punt returns were beautiful to behold. He passed and kicked with precision and, in fact, conducted himself like one would reasonably expect a great football player being paid for his services to conduct himself.[11]

Major league baseball players indeed played at levels clearly above what the best college and amateur clubs could ever show. It would be many years before professional football could present such a contrast between themselves and the best of the college game. In those days exhibitions between pro and college teams, or games between professionals and aggregates of college all-stars were common, and gaps between the two supposed levels were often not apparent. So it was natural for some writers to sniff indignantly at any posturings of superior professionalism. If in the process of such expression a snooty reporter could use the performance of a black man to underscore his point, so much the better. Likely, the Chicago journalist did not care about any residual effects his words could have, but his barbs may have exacerbated tensions between Lillard and some white players and coaches in the league.

African-American newspapers could have been expected to give highlighted coverage to a player like Lillard, and indeed, in regard to the Bears-Cardinals game, the *Chicago Defender* wrote that Lillard "was the whole show and with his remarkable kicking and return of punts saved a show that was otherwise dull."[12] White readers and football people could discount the coverage of the *Defender*, assuming they were even aware of it, but the *Herald and Examiner* was a mainstream paper. Their coverage spoke well of Lillard's contributions. In an age when any show of pride was dangerous for a black man, particularly one in a position of such visibility as an athlete, the press coverage Lillard received may have further served to aggravate the suspicions and tensions some players and coaches harbored about their new star. At the end of October, recalling how Lillard had stolen the show against Grange, Nagurski, and the rest of the Bears (as well as how that fall another black player named Fitzhugh Lyons was starring for Indiana University), the *Chicago Defender* conjectured how such quality speaks further for the integration of major league baseball. "If Lillard, a Race boy, is good enough to play in the winter sport, we see no reason why he should not be eligible in the summer pastime before the same fandom ..., [for] truly there is little difference between the fandom which supports professional football and those seen at baseball games." The integration of baseball was always "the prize" on which African American sports journalists fixed their attention. Everyone knew that was the salient point of resistance, one which, if conquered, could lead to the crumbling of a whole host of Jim Crow traditions.[13]

Lillard's stardom was providing hope, but the expression of such hope also made many others feel discomfort. In such an environment, hints of "attitude" from a man like Lillard that were anything other than submissive would be greatly magnified in the minds of any prejudiced party. Lillard was a man who was anything but submissive.

The Cardinals' next outing was against the league's new Boston team, first named the Braves.* Here Chicago won decisively, shutting out Boston 9–0. Again Lillard starred. Boston papers praised him. The *Globe* gave Lillard headline coverage, telling how the "Negro star ... thrills 18,000 by dazzling runs." Another Boston columnist wrote that, "Lillard is not only the ace of the Cardinal backfield but he is one of the greatest all-around players that has ever displayed his wares on any gridiron in this section of the country." The *Chicago Tribune* was also effusive: "Joe Lillard, negro halfback star, led the Cardinals to their touchdown and stood out in general.... Lillard virtually took possession of the game right from the start."[14] In the next week, in a non-league game with Providence (who had dropped out of the NFL that year), the Cards won 7–0, and, according to the *Tribune*, Lillard was instrumental on defense, intercepting three Providence passes at the goal line.[15]

Lillard's contributions to Chicago's newly founded success were obvious and undeniable. Whatever the personality dynamics between Lillard and his teammates, or between Lillard and his coaches, they would likely have been matters of varied opinion, even if the many parties were available for interviews (as is the case when personality issues arise on teams in more recent eras of microscopic media attention). To believe that race played no role, however, would be naive in the extreme.

Whatever the precise issues, Lillard began to fade from visibility, and with his eclipse, the Cardinals' standing in the league dropped quickly. With Lillard starring, the Cards were in contention for the league lead. After their victory against lowly Brooklyn (3–9 that year) in the week after the Providence game, the Cardinals would neither win nor even tie a single game for the rest of the season.

Lillard saw little to no action in the Brooklyn game at the end of October. Some cast this as an extension of conflicts between Lillard and his coach, and that may have been the case, but in the Cardinals'

A group of Boston businessmen, including George Preston Marshall, had bought the remnants of a failed NFL franchise in Newark, N.J. (1–10–1 in 1930; dormant in '31). Moving the franchise to Boston, and seeking to build on the existing baseball fan-base, they named the team the Braves. New York's NFL had done the same with their team—the Giants. Pittsburgh's NFL team was first called the Pirates, a team in Cincinnati back then took the name Reds, and one in Brooklyn naturally called themselves the Dodgers. George Halas had cutely varied the name Cubs into the more ferocious Bears. In the following season, Marshall would adjust the Braves similarly; he had then gained single-handed control of the team and renamed them the Redskins. In 1937 he moved them to Washington, D.C.

next game, a loss to Green Bay, Lillard did play, and the *Chicago Tribune* made a point of noting that Lillard was playing with the handicap of an injured ankle. Injuries alone could be an explanation of Lillard's diminution, but injuries themselves could also have compounded the mix of tensions, as some coaches and players will be predisposed to see someone with an injury failing to show the right toughness to play through a problem, and rhetoric about this can easily be laced with prejudiced stereotypes. One of Lillard's coaches with the Cardinals, Paul Schlissler, conceded that opponents were primed for Lillard, both because he was the star and because he was black. "He was a marked man, and I don't mean that just the Southern boys took it out on him either; after a while whole teams, Northern and Southern alike, would give Joe the works, and I would have to take him out."[16] Whatever the combinations of injuries and racial tensions, in late 1932 Lillard saw little action.

With the Cardinals playing two games in a row in New York, first with Brooklyn and then against the Staten Island Stapletons, the team remained in the East for the week. Lillard missed an evening meeting that week and was fined $50, a rather stiff fine for those days. In covering the weekend's loss to the Stapletons, the Chicago papers made no mention of Lillard ever appearing.[17]

The Cardinals went back to Chicago and played the Bears four days later in a special Thanksgiving Day city championship game. Some writers have alleged that Lillard was dropped from the team by this point.[18] The *Tribune*, meanwhile, made no mention of Lillard being suspended, and in their pre-game coverage of the Thanksgiving game with the Bears, the *Herald and Examiner* mentioned that Lillard was hurt and "doubtful" to see action. Whether suspended or hurt, Lillard was certainly seeing no action, and, not coincidentally, the Cardinals' fortunes were plummeting. The Bears clobbered them 34–0. Three days later the Cardinals hosted the Boston team Lillard had helped shut out earlier in the season. This time Boston won 8–6.

No matter when the precise point of the suspension, Lillard was indeed dropped from the team. The *Defender* cited the prejudice of Cardinals' head coach Jack Chevigny as the cause. Chevigny had formerly been at Notre Dame, and, as the *Defender* noted, "they don't use Race boys up at Notre Dame." The newspapers never interviewed other players about the matter, nor did they ask Lillard or Chevigny. The Cardinals were a lesser team in a professional sport that had but a marginal hold on the American sports world anyway. Even in Chicago, the Bears would always get the major media attention. So the suspension of even such a standout player as Lillard passed with virtually no notice.

Lillard spent some of the winter months playing some more professional basketball for Abe Saperstein's Savoy Big Five. In the spring and summer he played professional baseball with the Negro American League's Chicago Giants. His athletic ability and versatility were indeed remarkable.

Lillard would come back to play for the Chicago Cardinals in the summer of 1933. African American writers like Al Monroe of the *Chicago Defender* and Wendell Smith of the *Pittsburgh Courier* had lamented that the already minimal visibility black athletes had in professional football was fading. They continued to hope that lesser sports like football and basketball could serve as points of leverage for doors to open in baseball, the integration of which, they continued to believe, would have profound effects upon the overall patterns and hold of Jim Crow in American society. These writers and many others thus believed it was essential for individuals like Lillard to do all they could to stay in their respective professional games. Echoing the views of such giants as Booker T. Washington, they urged accommodation, that people in positions like Lillard's seek to be manipulative rather than confrontational; "learn to play upon the vanity" of the powerful was one of Al Monroe's explicit prescriptions. The Cardinals' public relations officer, Rocky Wolfe, commented that Lillard was anything but humble: "Football players, like anyone else, will always be jealous, but a fellow can always clear up such a situation by living, walking, and breathing in a manner that does not bespeak supremacy—a thing Lillard hasn't learned."[19]

As people look back upon such ideas, it is all too easy to sniff and cast these thoughts as more than a bit Uncle Tom-ish. But, as it was for Booker T. Washington earlier in the century, the era was one of such extreme difficulties that almost any form of defiance meant certain defeat. Writers like Al Monroe were asking for something that went beyond mere meekness or defiance, it required true strengths of character and temperament, just as the ideas of Mahatma Gandhi and Martin Luther King about passive resistance meant much more than mere passivity. Such tall orders did demand much. For some people, apparently like Lillard, it demanded things their personalities could not summon. Lillard had more of a brooding nature. If hit, he hit back. A white athlete with such a nature was and is usually dubbed "intense" or "fiery." If people refer to such white athletes as "animals," invariably they do so with a smile. The double standard at work here is clear, as blacks with such natures engendered fear. Fritz

Pollard had the temperament to make strides for many. Lillard was endowed with as much or more athletic ability but a very different nature. Much like Muhammad Ali, Paul Robeson seemed able to combine a controlled inner rage with a judiciousness of temperament, calculating instinct, and brilliance to be able to channel his feelings and take his agenda to such broader political levels that he could not be summarily dismissed and squashed as could a mere athlete. Lillard, meanwhile, had a definite edge, and, as Ray Kemp (the only other African American in the NFL at that time) recalled, Lillard "was an angry young man, and the players on other teams knew what would set him off."[20]

As Lillard began playing again for the Chicago Cardinals in 1933, one other African American, Ray Kemp, also tried out for a spot in the NFL on the squad of a new team in the league, the Pittsburgh Pirates. (Renamed the Steelers in 1940, they still kept the baseball Pirates' black and gold team colors.) Kemp had been a standout at tackle at nearby Duquesne University, and he proved more than worthy of making the team. As with regard to Lillard, writers for African American papers were happy, but nervous. Unceasingly, they wanted people like Kemp and Lillard to keep alive the hope of blacks penetrating the professional sports world as part of an overall desire to see the patterns of Jim Crow crumble. Kemp played well for the Pirates, but he found himself suspended after three games, though later he was reinstated for the final three weeks of the season.

Rumors flew that Kemp's suspension had been imposed because he had gotten into a fight during a game. Caring deeply, and somewhat nervously, about the tenuous status of African Americans in sports, the *Pittsburgh Courier* did not attempt to question the story. They were silent. Ironically, it was the city's main white newspaper, the *Post Gazette*, that denied Kemp had ever gotten into any such fracas. Why then had Kemp been suspended? The *Courier* looked into the matter. They encountered a somewhat defensive and not fully logical Art Rooney, the team's founder and president. Rooney was effusive about how the local fans all heralded Kemp's sterling play at tackle. Rooney went on about Kemp being one of the strong points of the Pirates' forward wall. But, said Rooney, a new league rule demanded that squads be cut to twenty-two players after the third game, a rule that Rooney said hit him "like an thunderbolt." Rooney was likely being a trifle disingenuous here, as he was part of all owners' meetings and was involved in discussions of all such rule changes from start to finish; his disingenuousness here could indicate that he may have been one of the initiators of the change, as his team's finances were not the strongest. Unlike some other NFL owners, Rooney had been having difficulties with the proprietors of his city's baseball stadium, Forbes Field, where he played his home games. The Forbes Field management would grant Rooney the revenues from ticket sales to his games, but he could get no other revenues from such money makers as food and beverage concessions. This put Rooney on even thinner financial ice.

The only problem about Kemp at which Rooney hinted was that relations between Kemp and his coach, Jap Douds, "were somewhat strained." Rooney never went into any specifics about it. Beyond that, Rooney attempted to explain that there were two other men on the team, each with two years of professional experience—"the coach ... and a first string man who naturally would get the preference over Ray." Noting that while the team found no fault with Kemp's playing ability, Rooney emphasized that Kemp was a sub, not a regular. But Rooney had said what a strong point Kemp was on the Pirate line, and he went on to say that while Kemp did not start, he "usually played most of the game." That certainly defines him as a "regular." (As Red Auerbach of the Boston Celtics once noted, "it's not who starts the game, it's who finishes it.") Rooney went on to claim that he had secured Kemp a berth on the Philadelphia team, but said that Kemp refused it.

Rooney's explanation did not fully make sense. The twenty-two man rule hardly hit him suddenly. Why, as well, did Rooney judge Kemp's situation only in relation to the tenure of the coach and to one other player? This was never clear. Rooney did release four other players as well as Kemp—guard Howard Letsinger, halfback Jim Tanguay, and two quarterbacks, Butch Kottler and George Shaffer. But these players definitely were substitutes, and they were not rehired, as Kemp was later in the season. Meanwhile, aside from the two men Rooney mentioned he would keep, the obvious question was: what of the other 20 men kept on the squad, many of whom had logged less playing time than Kemp? It is not difficult to believe that Kemp, the only truly quality player to be cut, fell victim, at least in part, to the concern that blue-collar fans would resent the continued employment of a black man while whites were being laid off, especially in the fall of 1933 when the Depression in industrial Pittsburgh was at its absolute nadir. While Kemp's layoff was problematic, and although he was brought back late in the fall, when the season ended and the league's owners met, a color bar ended Kemp's pro football career permanently.

In subsequent generations, black players for the Pittsburgh Steelers came to love Art Rooney deeply. Tackle and later assistant coach Joe Greene held such an affection for the man that he could be moved to tears when reminiscing about him. Doubtlessly, Rooney had a capacity to grow beyond the prejudices which had dominated his earlier days. Additionally, back in the early 1930s, being new to a league that was always on the brink of financial failure, he wanted to fit in with his new brethren and not rock the boat over such a potentially corrosive issue as race, especially since some owners, like Boston's George Preston Marshall, harbored virulently hateful attitudes anyway. When the other owners imposed a color barrier, Rooney complied without objection, doubtlessly continuing to remember as well that his city's working class fans would readily resent a maintaining of the employment of a black man while others, amidst a depression, were being laid off.

Amidst Ray Kemp's sad vicissitudes, Joe Lillard's final year with the Cardinals again showed his undeniable talent, his endless bad fortune, and the utter haplessness of the Chicago Cardinals team. A bright spot appeared at first. Racist coach Jack Chevigny had been let go, replaced by the less abrasive Paul Schlissler. Schlissler was willing to go with such a talented player as Lillard.

Schlissler's Cardinals' first outing was against Pittsburgh. Lillard starred as the Cardinals built up a 13–0 lead by halftime. The Pirates came back to win 14–13, and the papers made a point of mentioning that Lillard's missing an extra point gave Pittsburgh the edge.[21] The 1933 season marked the point when footballs were no longer the fat round objects they had been since the original inflated pig's bladders of the late nineteenth/early twentieth century. More oblong, like the modern football, the balls were easier to pass but bounced much more unpredictably. This made drop kicks more difficult, and field goal and point-after-touchdown misses became more common. (By 1938, because of the changed shape of the ball, the drop kick ceased to be used for field goals or extra points.) Lillard's missed PAT against Pittsburgh therefore was not unusual. Nonetheless, he took the blame for the team's loss.

During the 1933 season, Lillard's fearsome image took on new features, with some "extra-curricular's" which began with the Pittsburgh game. Late in that game, Pirate fullback and linebacker Tony Holm squared off against Lillard, and both appeared ready to fight. The Pittsburgh papers stated that others started the trouble, but as is usually the case in a sports brawl, the second and third combatants invariably draw the officials' attention. Holm and Lillard were ejected, and without Lillard in the game, Pittsburgh was able to come back and win. The following week, in a game against the Spartans of Portsmouth, Ohio, Chicago lost 7–6. Lillard was again outstanding. He threw for the Cardinals' one touchdown, and he ran and passed effectively throughout the game. But the papers noted that Lillard's extra point was blocked and that Portsmouth's winning score had been set up by a poor Lillard punt which gave the Spartans the ball on Chicago's 20-yard line. Lillard dominated the team to such a degree that, whenever the Cardinals played, reporters were apt to scour all aspects of his performances. The star of a lousy team, he became the reason for their successes and their failures. During the Portsmouth game, another fight also broke out. This fight reached such proportions that fans spilled onto the field to take part, causing not just the referees but the Portsmouth police to enter and restore order. Storm clouds again appeared to follow Lillard wherever he went.

More the typical mill town of the old–NFL type, full of migrated Southern blue collar workers, Portsmouth, Ohio, displayed some of the most blatantly racist attitudes. With Lillard on the field, racial taunts from the stands (which were closer to the field than were those in big-city stadiums) were numerous and vicious. The sports reporter for the *Portsmouth Times*, Lynn Wittenberg, recognized Lillard's "brilliant" play, but he detailed his description with language of how Lillard "roamed the field like an ebony panther ... and proved a dark menace to the Spartans." Throughout his coverage, Wittenberg continued to pepper his prose with words and phrases like "dark menace," "dusky," "Ebony," "an ebony-hued bird in the Red Bird covery," and "an Ethiopian in the wood pile." Wittenberg claimed that Lillard had instigated several fights. He wrote fearfully of how greater levels of violence seemed ready to burst forth at any moment, and concluded that, "it might be better if Portsmouth and the Cardinals do not meet, especially here."[22] Portsmouth was probably the worst environment in which Lillard played in 1932–33, but it was only an exaggerated form of what he was experiencing everywhere else. Because the Cardinals were also one of, if not *the* worst team in the league, there was no "comfort zone" for Lillard and his teammates throughout the season that winning games could have provided.

The next week's game against the new Cincinnati Reds was a tense affair between two very weak teams. It was scoreless well into the fourth quarter. Then Lillard led a Cardinal march down the field with a key nine yard run and twenty-five yard pass completion. This set him up to kick a field goal, which proved the only score of the whole game. Cincinnati's sports reporter, Lou Smith, praised Lillard's performance: "All in all he was the best back this writer has seen in many a day."[23] Cincinnati's offense, meanwhile, was utterly anemic; they would score but three points in their first six games that season. The Cardinals were no better. Their 3–0 victory over Cincinnati would prove their only win all season.

When lousy teams square off in a tense game, frustrations are apt to erupt. And when Lillard kicked the field goal, Cincinnati knew they were done. Upset over Lillard's field goal, Cincinnati's big guard, Les Caywood (only 16 players in the entire league weighed more than he), "decided," according to the *Chicago Defender*, "to dim Joe's eyesight, if not the glory that was already the property of the Windy City flash. So Caywood sent a left to Lillard's face but received a mighty left in return." The *Tribune* confirmed that Caywood was the clear instigator here. The only discrepancy between their story and the *Defender's* was that the *Tribune* claimed Lillard had landed not a left but "a right uppercut to Lester's prominent chin." The bigger Caywood then knocked Lillard to the turf. The referees intervened and both players were ejected. That marked three games in a row in which Lillard and extra-curricular violence had been on the same field. The following week marked the point when the league demanded that rosters be cut to twenty-two players. While the Pittsburgh Pirates suspended Ray Kemp, Lillard, though controversial, was obviously too valuable for the Cardinals to cut. Besides, the next week was a big game against the rival Bears.[24]

In the previous year's muddy 0–0 tie between the Cardinals and the Bears, Lillard had made local heroes like Red Grange look bad in the eyes of reporters. George Halas and the Bears did not want that to happen again. The game saw the Bears score two touchdowns (they missed both conversions), while the Cardinals could tally but one Lillard field goal. Comfortably ahead in the fourth quarter, the Bears punted, with Lillard back to field it. Lillard caught the ball and began running. The Cardinals hit their blocks just right. Lillard broke free, and no one would catch him. Punt returns for touchdowns are rare in the modern game. Back then they were even more unusual, and Lillard's 53 yard return received raves. Even though the Bears held on to win the game 12–9 (after the run, Lillard missed the conversion), newspapers focused on Lillard's feat. The *Chicago Defender* wrote of how Lillard was "all over the field" and made the Bears "look miserably bad." The *Defender* snapped a marvelous photograph of Lillard during is long punt return, just as he sped past the Bears' last defender, who was none other than the great Red Grange. Grange actually gave up running as Lillard ran away from him. He knew he had been bested. The *Defender* chortled with a mocking headline over

Joe Lillard. A virtual one-man team for the otherwise hapless Chicago Cardinals of the early 1930s, Lillard was a leading runner, passer, receiver, punter, place kicker, return man, and defensive back. Here Lillard is returning a punt for a touchdown against the Bears (with Red Grange trying to tackle him). After the 1933 season, despite undeniable talents, Lillard would not be allowed to play with any NFL team.

the picture, intentional in its double entendre: "Sorry Red, see you on the other side of the goal." Enduring so many journalists' wisecracks about racial characteristics, the *Defender* could not resist a jab of their own against Grange, reporting how Lillard had "side-stepped the 'Sorrel Top.'"[25]

There was something poetic in the great player of the 1920s now falling just short as he attempted to keep up with a new star in a new decade. Rather than just let such progress evolve, however, the corporate leadership of the NFL had a much more controlled form of "evolution" in mind for the development of talent in professional football. No matter his talent, Joe Lillard was not to be a part of their plans.

It was in this same era of the 1930s that novelist Richard Wright attempted to confront America not merely with questions of racial injustice, which others had been raising for decades, but with the point that some African Americans with whom they would have to contend would not always be noble and non-threatening. Compared with the likes of Fritz Pollard, Joe Lillard was such an individual, though not so starkly fearful as a figure like boxer Jack Johnson. Lillard's talent was undeniable, and his personae left less room for whites to look for

some sort of comfort zone. In a later time, compared with the likes of
football players like Duane Thomas or Jack Tatum, Lillard would
hardly have been considered extreme. But in the trying times of Depres-
sion/Jim Crow America he was up against quite a stacked deck.

Save for a pathetic 0–0 tie against Boston on the last day of the
season, the Cardinals lost all of their remaining games of 1933, including a rematch with lowly Cincinnati. In a game against Green Bay on
November 5, Lillard appeared to give Chicago a perfect opportunity
to score when he punted the ball 82 yards to the Packers one-yard
line, with the ball first ruled to have grazed a Packer, hence the down-
ing giving Chicago the possession. The Packers protested vehemently
and a fight broke out. The referees reversed their call. Chicago lost
their scoring opportunity, and Lillard was at least tangentially impli-
cated in Chicago's fourth on-field fight of the season. Lillard kicked
but two more field goals all season, and he scored only one more
touchdown—on the Thanksgiving Day game against the Bears. As in
'32 and earlier that season, George Halas and the Bears could beat
the Cardinals, but Lillard was another matter. Halas was never one
to take any slight or defeat with much grace, nor was he one to hes-
itate if he could get away with a dirty trick against any opposition,
especially if his fellow team owners were with him. Halas likely
resented Lillard, who stood defiantly against Halas' total domination
of Chicago football. Getting rid of him made sense to such a parsimonious man, and this would indeed happen.

As the Cards' pathetic season wore on, Lillard's quality was undeniable; "Easily the best halfback in football," the *Chicago Defender*
called him.[26] Still, as the losing season wound down, Lillard appeared
to receive less playing time. Whether it was injury, attitude (perceived
or real), coaching/teammate prejudice, or a combination of such factors, Lillard appeared on the outs. The fights, even those that were
not his fault, had highlighted his "bad" image. His coach, Paul
Schlissler, commented that Lillard was a marked man. With player
after player taking shots at him, Schlissler felt compelled to bench
him. Lillard was clearly the best player on the team, but late in the
season he was no longer starting. In the final game against Boston,
Lillard scooped up a fumble and returned it 85 yards for an apparent
touchdown that would have won the game. But the referees called the
score back, ruling Lillard down. This was a dubious call, as until the
1950s a runner could fall yet get back up if no one was on top of him.
But here Lillard was ruled down, and, in more ways than one, he certainly was.

Whether the somewhat unfairly drawn, sinister image of a star like Lillard was particularly motivating, or whether such an individual image simply added a bit of verbiage to the mix, the NFL owners met after the 1933 season and dealt with the race question. They left no written records of their meetings, but it is abundantly clear that at the end of the 1933 season they chose to ban African Americans from the league. With shameful disingenuousness, George Halas denied that any sort of ban had been established. When asked why blacks did not appear in the NFL from 1933 to 1946, Halas mused pathetically that the game "didn't have the appeal to black players at the time." Of note here is the fact that Halas did not refer "to black athletes" but "to black players." (Was he referring to baseball players?) His statement was so transparent in its flaws. Elsewhere a reporter once asked Halas about the absence of blacks in the NFL in the '30s and '40s, and Halas answered with mock surprise: "I don't know! Probably it was due to the fact that no great players were in the colleges then[!]. That could be the reason. But I've never given this a thought until you mentioned it. At no time has it ever been brought up. Isn't that strange?"[27] Like Art Rooney, Halas certainly changed his tune about black football players later in life and engendered the love of many, including, for example, Gayle Sayers. But there is no way to candy coat what he did in the 1930s, and his clumsy, inept verbal cover-ups speak poignantly of his immoral deeds.

In regard to the drawing of the racial bar, other owners provided points of evidence. Art Rooney said, with a combination of psychological denial and legalistic honesty, that he felt there never was any "racial bias." There may or may not have been provable bias, but, while smoking guns in regard to what lies in someone's heart can seldom be found, Rooney side-stepped the question of a "ban," and the omission was revealing. Tex Schramm, who later ran both the Los Angeles Rams and the Dallas Cowboys, was more honest about the attitude about signing blacks in the '30s and early '40s: "You just didn't do it," he recalled. Schramm's point, of course, contradicts Halas's assertions that the game must not have had any appeal to blacks. The point was that the talent was there, and everyone knew it. Moreover, since owners had previously signed talented African American football players, and then reached a point where one just did not do it, logically there had to have been a point when people made the choice to stop doing what they had been doing. This is exactly what occurred after the 1933 season.[28]

George Preston Marshall, who had gained full control of the Boston Braves after 1932, was a leader among the NFL owners. It was Marshall who determined the effective way to narrow and structure the league into two divisions and stage a league championship game between division winners. Marshall was also the first owner skilled at marketing the game. He was a showman. He invented the half-time show. He staged team parades. His team had the NFL's first "fight song," one still in use. He loved to appear in fancy clothes and to advertise his team with pretty girls. (One retired reporter from the now defunct *Washington Star* commented on how Marshall also had more than team advertising in mind with his employment of pretty girls.)[29] But the point was that Marshall's tactics worked. He helped nudge the game beyond the image of beer guzzling steel workers and coal miners, and sought to make it an acceptable enjoyment for a wider swath of the public. It was still a most crass type of appeal, but it was an effective one.

In the context of Marshall's crass nature and marketing methods, a decided racism permeated his character. As he persuaded the NFL owners to adopt his organization scheme, and showed them, by example, how to market the game, he could argue, without skipping a beat, that black players would detract from the efforts to broaden the game's appeal. These views were anything but out of step with the popular sensibilities of the day. Black communities of the time were of no interest to a man like Marshall. Their capital was nil compared to what Marshall reckoned he could pull out of the sports public's mainstream. And liberal thinking whites apt to take political exception to Marshall's methods and attitudes were hardly the main clientele among potential pro football fans. The Eleanor Roosevelts of America were concerned about racial injustice, but not in professional football, so Marshall felt no need to pay attention to such people. Marshall thus knew how to define and exploit a market niche. And as he and others went after it, the African American presence in professional football was cut away. In 1934 the "weak string," as the *Chicago Defender*'s Al Monroe called the remnant of black presence in the NFL, was cut. There was nothing anyone could conceivably do about it, and, given the despair that prevailed in the country at that point, few could be convinced that the segregation was going to be anything but permanent.

Seven

The Segregation Years

With the realignment of 1933, many National Football League owners found financial success. Fans gained a stronger, albeit not completely true, sense of the league representing the best the game of football had to offer. The League also presented an exciting two-division alignment that produced a national championship every December. Despite the Depression, fans bought more tickets. Teams caught some of the mood of the times and built stronger bases of fan support. Philadelphia, for example, named their team "the Eagles." This was done intentionally to capitalize upon the spirit of President Roosevelt's New Deal, specifically his National Recovery Administration, whose symbol, "the Blue Eagle," proudly proclaimed any business displaying it to be doing its part in the U.S. government's effort to revive the economy and the nation. The Philadelphia Eagles became popular, as did most of the league's teams. Nine of the ten NFL teams survived the depression decade, and league prestige grew considerably. The one failure was the Cincinnati Reds. They had only begun play in 1933. In two seasons their records were 3–6 and 0–8. During the '34 season they stopped playing in Cincinnati. For the remainder of 1934 they relocated to St. Louis, calling themselves "the Gunners," but they failed there too. The league then played with nine teams. In 1937 they rebalanced themselves—five in the East, five in the West—with a tenth team, the Rams, who began play for eight seasons in Cleveland.

Even in the years of World War II, the league continued to play, despite acute manpower shortages. George Halas drew players out of retirement, Bronko Nagurski most famously, to bolster his squad's sagging ranks. The Bears continued to thrive, but many teams had a rocky time of it during the war. The Cleveland Rams had to disband for one year, 1943. That same year, the Philadelphia and Pittsburgh squads had to merge, calling themselves the "Steagles." In 1944 the

Eagles went solo again; Pittsburgh then temporarily joined forces with the Chicago Cardinals. This time they were known as the "Carpets," and they lost every game, with only one even being close. Also in 1944, the usually last-place Brooklyn Dodgers renamed themselves the Tigers. Hoping for some kind of magic with a new name, they also proceeded to lose every game. In 1945 singer Kate Smith, of "God Bless America" fame, bought the remnants of the Brooklyn club and moved them to Boston, merging them with a one-year-old NFL club she owned known as the Yanks. As the Yanks, they played in Boston from 1945 through 1948. (In 1949 they moved back to New York and took the name "Bulldogs," as a professional football team called the Yankees already existed in New York within a new league, the All America Conference. In 1950 and '51, with the folding of that All America Football Conference, the Bulldogs reclaimed the name Yanks but continued to struggle against a longer established, more popular, and better New York team. In 1952 they moved to Dallas, adopting the name Texans. In Texas they nearly folded, playing the second half of their season strictly on the road and practicing in Hershey, Pennsylvania. In 1953 the remnants of the Texans relocated to Baltimore, accepting the city's previously used pro football team name of Colts. They moved from there to Indianapolis late one evening in 1984.)

Amidst these many struggles for survival, an obvious key for any franchise's success was to provide local fans with a quality team. The successful teams of the 1933–45 era, like the New York Giants, Chicago Bears, Washington Redskins, and the Green Bay Packers, succeeded with fan support in this simple way—they won a lot of football games. Despite this obvious avenue for success, and, even more, despite the incredible shortages of players during the war years, the league owners' agreement banning the hiring of African Americans held tightly. Even the marginal teams like Brooklyn and Pittsburgh would not break it. While George Halas insincerely conjectured that there were no black players in the NFL from 1933 to 1946 because the game "didn't have the appeal to black players at the time," any cursory look at the game reveals not only an appeal but a great cache of talent. Art Rooney also feebly attempted to claim that the lack of good scouting systems made finding African American football talent too difficult for NFL teams. The fact was, however, that black players were visible, and white talent was being found on many of the same fields where blacks played.

In baseball everyone knew that the ranks of the African American leagues were packed with incredibly talented men. The knowledge here stemmed from more than the mere awareness of the segregated black leagues, though that in itself provided ample evidence of the greatness that was available. Outside the segregated play of the regular major league seasons, after most seasons, teams of white and black players used to tour the country. From October to December, racially mixed teams toured, following the passing of the year's remaining warm weather from North to South. In the winter many of these players, black and white, would also venture to Mexico or to the Caribbean for more ball playing.[1] Pitchers like Bob Feller knew of the greatness of Josh Gibson first-hand, they had faced one another many times.

After winter ball, black and white players would re-segregate for spring training in March, though even then there would be some racially mixed exhibitions. Before the 1937 season, for example, representatives of the Pittsburgh Pirates ventured across town to watch some workouts by the city's two "colored" teams, the Homestead Grays and the Pittsburgh Crawfords. After witnessing the likes of Josh Gibson, "Cool Papa" Bell, Oscar Charleston, and Buck Leonard, Pirates officials suddenly realized that they "weren't going to have time" to play anyone before the season opener. (New York was not the only city in that era with three big league baseball teams; and in late-1930s Pittsburgh, the Pirates probably ran a strong third.)

Everyone in baseball knew of the talents that existed among African American players. But with a most unrelenting Commissioner in Judge Landis, the Jim Crow system in major league baseball could not be broken. One major absurdity in the barrier's maintenance was how it particularly affected incessantly lowly clubs like the Washington Senators and the St. Louis Browns. The signing of stars from the black leagues could have shown the cellar dwellers a road upward. Dizzy Dean once remarked that if the already powerful St. Louis Cardinals of the mid-1930s would sign Josh Gibson and Satchel Paige, the Cardinals could wrap up the pennant in July, and everyone could go fishing for a few months before the World Series. Dean was only slightly exaggerating, and the inclusion of a Gibson or a Paige in a team like Washington would have indeed had a huge impact. The fact that the leaders of the worst baseball clubs would not, could not, venture onto such a pathway to excellence, and preferred to be perennial league doormats, speaks poignantly to the depths to which the influence of Jim Crow, and the Commissioner's office, penetrated.

While football did not have the sophisticated structure of black and white baseball, the visibility of African American talent was present as well. When Art Rooney said that NFL clubs hadn't sufficient scouting systems to be aware of African American talent, and when

George Halas declared that blacks were just not interested in football, they were simply lying, and they knew it. There were two avenues through which African American football players continued to display their talents, and both were well known to all informed football men—the second-tier professional circuits and the college ranks.

Led by Fritz Pollard, some enterprising African American football people endeavored to create some professional and semi-professional football circuits. With players involved like Joe Lillard, Inky Williams, Sol Butler, Duke Slater, and Pollard himself, any legitimate football person knew that some valuable talent labored in these leagues. Major league baseball had been segregated since the 1880s, and the long interregnum from that point until Jackie Robinson's first playing for Brooklyn in 1947 gave sufficient time for the full development of black baseball leagues. Pro football started later, segregated later, and did so for a shorter era, one which happened, as well, to involve both the Great Depression and World War II. All this combined to make the development of full professional black football leagues much more difficult. Yet some teams did crop up, usually for brief stints. Three teams appeared in Tennessee, for example—the Nashville Purple Pirates, the Knoxville Black Vols, and the Chattanooga Ramblers. They played one another and simply put out the proverbial "welcome mat," offering to play all comers, black or white. The enthusiasm was there, but none of the teams made much of a go of it financially.[2]

In Chicago, Fritz Pollard attempted to start a football team called the Black Hawks. Pollard played as well as coached, and he employed such stars as Duke Slater and Joe Lillard. The team did not go too far financially, suffering poor gate attendance as well as minimal press coverage, even in African American newspapers. They disbanded in 1931.[3]

In 1935 a team began to play in New York called the Harlem Brown Bombers. They took their name in an attempt to draw upon the popularity of heavyweight boxing champion Joe Louis, as Brown Bomber was his well-known nickname. Fritz Pollard coached the team. The Brown Bombers received slightly better press coverage than Coach Pollard had found in Chicago with the Black Hawks, but gate attendance was still poor. The team played some good football, beating quality teams in New York, New Jersey, and New England. Joe Lillard put in several appearances with them, as did some other top players neglected by the NFL. Many also came out of the largely unnoticed talent pools of the nation's black colleges, another source that the NFL would naturally not touch. But the Bombers also failed to make any significant profits.

Other black teams cropped up, often in financial competition with one another. In addition to New York's Brown Bombers, the city boasted the Black Yankees, and Chicago was home to the Comets, later called the Panthers. At times both the Comets and Fritz Pollard's various clubs played white teams. In 1938 Pollard's Bombers played in a racially integrated semipro league. Pollard hoped the examples of black and white athletes playing together without serious incidents would help reopen the door to the NFL, as well as provide an example for steps toward more general integration in American society. But these changes were not to occur. Pollard's efforts were substantive and noble, but few with any political influence cared to take any notice, let alone draw any political or moral lessons.

As business enterprises, professional football team efforts by people like Pollard were further handicapped by the fact that football had not yet penetrated the sporting life of the United States. Any sports fans of post-1950 vintage can easily forget the point that before 1945 no American team sport besides baseball had successfully gained much of a national following. The media were too meager in scope, and any other game, be it basketball, football, or hockey, had, outside of a few regions, never penetrated the playing habits of the youth or fired the imaginations of a sufficiently sizable mass to yield any major following of teams or idolatry of star performers.

Besides baseball, the only team sport which had some national presence was college football. Even here, though, the fan support at this time was largely regional. In parts of the nation, a few African Americans starred for some colleges and universities, but, as with other college sports even in later decades, college football was often not only the apex but the end of the line for individual players. Within this more restricted genre, the black college football star had an even more imposing ceiling over him than did his white counterpart.[4]

While the struggling black professional teams of the segregation years gave outlets for such established talents as Joe Lillard, Duke Slater, and Fritz Pollard, they also provided room for some new talents. Many of these exceptional athletes came out of the college ranks. Some had played with such notice that, had they been white, they would have clearly been snapped up by an NFL franchise. Moreover, the postures of NFL owners like Halas and Rooney notwithstanding, professional scouts certainly knew about many of the players. For some of the neglected stars, the black professional teams would provide them their only bit of limelight. For others, lucky to be the right age at a precipitous moment, the leagues and teams would be a waiting ground until the NFL finally came 'round to saner ways.

For the most part, the college game continued to maintain a higher visibility within each school's particular region than did the professional game. And out of the college ranks, contrary to the disingenuous views of people like George Halas and Art Rooney, African American talent continued to appear. The Midwest was known for particularly strong football in the Depression years. There, Indiana University boasted three gifted African American athletes at this time—Archie Harris, Fitzhugh Lyons, and Jesse Babb. Thomas Harding was a key player for Indianapolis's Butler University in 1937. Fritz Pollard, Jr., who first attended his father's alma mater Brown, starred at North Dakota from 1936 to 1938. At the University of Minnesota, Horace Bell, Elsworth Harpole, and Dwight Reed were all top players. The University of Iowa boasted several talented African American players, including Don Simmons, Windy Wallace and Homer Harris. Harris was elected the Iowa team's captain in 1938. Clarence Hinton played halfback for Northwestern from 1935 to 1937. One year behind Hinton, Bernard Jefferson was a true standout at halfback for Northwestern, and was one of the best runners in the Big Ten. Farther west, in the Pacific Coast Conference, Charles Russell and Hamilton Greene started for the University of Washington, as did Walter Gordon at the University of California—Berkeley.

Contrary to the notion that black players were simply invisible to NFL owners, the level of coverage all these teams had in their regional presses was such that there was no way any football scout who did little more than simply read the major newspapers could not have been aware of them. Had they been white, all of these players would have been recruited by NFL teams and at least given a tryout, especially Northwestern's Bernard Jefferson, who could possibly have become a professional star. Neither Jefferson nor any other of these athletes ever got a decent look from the pros, however.

Beyond even such quality players, several genuine African American stars dotted the college ranks in the 1930s. The NFL's refusal to give any of them a look was even more absurd. Brud Holland, for example, was an All-American running back at Cornell University, with the Ivy League then being a major college football division with enormous coverage in the Eastern press. Holland had played his high school ball in the nearby Upstate New York town of Auburn. There he gained such raves that the nearby Cornell coaches could not pass on him. Holland then became Cornell's first African American. Holland's position was end, and his catching and running became legendary. The "end-around" play was developed and first employed by Cornell's coaches specifically to utilize Holland's speed and power, and he could pull off the play like no other in his day. The exciting nature of the play helped make Holland a favorite with crowds. With such notice, professional football people had to know of Holland's exploits. Playing in New York, his game heroics drew plenty of coverage, not just in the black press or in upstate New York papers, but in the major New York City papers, including the *Times*.

Not since Paul Robeson's years at Rutgers had a black player received such raves in the New York papers as Holland. In a 1937 game against Colgate, Holland scored three touchdowns in the fourth quarter, two via end-around runs.[5] That same year, on a Thanksgiving Day game at the University of Pennsylvania, Holland again starred. After the game, thousands of Penn fans lined the walkway to shake Holland's hand. Holland received as many plaudits from the New York press as did such Ivy League contemporaries as Bob McLeod of Dartmouth and Sid Luckman of Columbia, both of whom went on to the NFL. Desperately wanting Luckman, George Halas had to finagle a deal whereby the lowly Pittsburgh Pirates selected Luckman early in the NFL draft and then traded him to Chicago (a little trick that would not be allowed in later times). In Chicago, Luckman went on to stardom, of course. Meanwhile, no pro team would chase or even consider the widely heralded Brud Holland.[6]

Another player who received much coverage in the Eastern press was Wilmeth Sidat-Singh, quarterback of Syracuse University from 1937 to 1939. (Sidat-Singh's name stemmed from the fact that, as an orphaned baby in Harlem, he was adopted by a Hindu-American family.) No less than Grantland Rice lauded Sidat-Singh's talents, describing his running and passing as that of "a human machine gun with a touch of the howitzer on the side." In a nine minute stretch in the fourth quarter of a game against Cornell in 1938, Sidat-Singh threw seven pass completions for 200 yards (including five in a row for 163 yards) and three touchdowns, giving Syracuse a come-back victory. Rice praised not just Sidat-Singh's obvious physical talents here, but also his coolness, accuracy, and timing, "something you'll seldom see," rhapsodized Rice. "A new forward pass hero slipped in front of the great white spotlight of fame at Syracuse today. The phenomenon of the rifle shot event went beyond Sid Luckman and Sammy Baugh [the latter already regarded as the best quarterback in the NFL]. His name is Wilmeth Sidat-Singh, a Negro boy from Harlem wearing an East Indian name with the deadly aim of Davy Crockett and Kit Carson."[7] It took many years for African Americans to penetrate the football ranks, and it took even longer for it to become acceptable for African Americans to play in such key positions as middle linebacker, free safety, and, most of all, quarterback. Yet back in the late 1930s Sidat-Singh was proving, to anyone who cared to observe, that race was no obstacle to success at such a position.

Although race was no obstacle to Sidat-Sing's work as a quarterback, racism was. In the 1937 season, for example, when Sidat-Singh and Syracuse visited the University of Maryland, their Southern host barred the quarterback from playing. Syracuse had to comply, or simply not play and forfeit. They chose to play, and without Sidat-Singh they lost. The next season Maryland visited Syracuse. This time, Syracuse controlled the ground rules. Sidat-Singh played (and then some). The whole Syracuse team was out for revenge, and at the end of the afternoon the score stood Syracuse 53, Maryland 0. After his Syracuse days were over, however, the race bar imposed in Maryland crashed down around Sidat-Singh. No NFL team would look at him; his playing days were over.[8]

The University of Iowa, while boasting such talented African American players as Homer Harris, Windy Wallace and Don Simmons, had a player of even more dazzling quality. This was Don Simmons' brother Ozzie. Ozzie Simmons had somewhat of a Joe Lillard reputation, one which may have extended from an uncompromising nature and, as well, from the pressures of prejudiced coaches and teammates. Simmons was a running back of such excellence that during his junior year at Iowa in 1935, the Associated Press voted him second-team All-American. Another All-American polling done among five of the nation's major college coaches completely overlooked Simmons, however. Prejudice may have played a role in the discrepancy here. Stories circulated throughout the Big Ten that Simmons was a "bad actor," that his teammates saw him as a selfish limelight lover, and that he caused such resentments that some linemen reportedly chose to block less intensely when his number was called. Indeed, when Simmons was a senior in 1936, he was, unquestionably, the team's star player. Rather than electing him captain, the Iowa squad chose instead to have no captain that season. Perhaps to show that they were personally but not racially motivated, at the beginning of the next season the team elected African American end Homer Harris to be their captain. With all the raves about his speed, savvy, and general athletic talent, Simmons expressed hopes of playing in the NFL. Again, despite obvious talent, no one would touch him.[9] Aside from cases involving military service or injury, when did anyone else earning All-America status fail to gain a tryout in the NFL? (Never!)

While opinions could have been rendered about Simmons' attitude to justify keeping him off a professional squad, he was, like Joe

Lillard, no more difficult a personality than many white NFL players of the day, let alone prima-donnas of any race in subsequent times. (In 1977, Tony Dorsett came out of the University of Pittsburgh with a similar reputation for ego, yet he starred for Dallas and is now in the Hall of Fame.) For many players, reputations for ego and nastiness can be assets, not liabilities. Furthermore, even if stories critical of Simmons were true, no such issues of personality were ever raised with respect to Brud Holland, Wilmeth Sidat-Singh, or Bernard Jefferson. Their exclusions from the NFL were unconscionable, and the added absurdity here was the degree to which the lesser teams of the league were cementing their lowly status by caving in to the demands of the owners of the more successful clubs not to have any truck with talented African American athletes.

Many historians of American slavery have noted one of its chief oddities—that, independent of its immorality, the institution was in many instances in the Old South not economically viable for the slave owner. Yet while slavery did not pay for itself, virtually all white Southerners clung to the institution anyway. Southern whites, including those who did not own slaves, often went to such lengths as the joining of militias to track down runaways, all with no pay and hence to the further diminution of the productivity of their own land. The sense of camaraderie with the few rich people who profited from the peculiar institution's maintenance made no rational economic sense, yet this was behavior that somehow gave psychic rewards which became central to the ongoing politics of the South. While the stakes were obviously not as significant, a similar mentality seems to have existed among sports team owners in Jim Crow America. In baseball, perennial doormat teams like the Washington Senators and the St. Louis Browns could never overtake a wealthy outfit like the New York Yankees. In season after season, furthermore, lowly clubs like the Browns would see sagging gate attendance imperil their finances. To offset such misfortunes toward a season's end, they would usually have to sell off some young, promising talent—and often to the Yankees. The latter's wealth then continued to compound and eclipse all rivals. With potential player pools kept limited, a way out of this cycle was to open the gates to talent that was being kept out. In the 1930s and 1940s, a tapping of the African American (or the equally untouched Latin American) talent pools was an obvious way to do this, but no one would dare try.

Just as Dizzy Dean knew that the likes of Josh Gibson and Satchel Paige could win pennants for any major league baseball team, the same was known about some available talent for professional football teams in the 1930s and '40s. This was especially poignant for such NFL lowlifes as the Chicago Cardinals and the Pittsburgh Pirates/Steelers. Joe Lillard, Ozzie Simmons, Brud Holland, and Wilmeth Sidat-Singh were right there in front of them; everybody knew it. But the self-destructive solidarity among the team owners overpowered all rational dictates. As historians have noted about slavery's defenders, and as psychologists note more generally, when a behavior persists that runs counter to all rational dictates, the defenders of the rationally indefensible will go to any length, including rage and violence, rather than admitting the folly of their ways and change. In such a dysfunctional state, furthermore, the meanest spirits usually dominate the order, for they usually have the sternest resolve.

In 1938 a crack in the NFL's racist wall appeared (and then quickly resealed). Since 1934, Chicago promoters had staged an annual game between the defending NFL champion and an aggregate of all-stars from the previous year's senior class of college players. It was a way of generating gate attendance for an additional game in the summer before league play commenced. As they have ever since, the NFL owners of the 1930s also staged pre-season, then called "exhibition," games, but the attendance was often low. Eager to have any sort of well-attended game boost revenues, George Halas agreed to another exhibition game that could draw substantial attendance. In this case he was to have his defending NFL champion Chicago Bears play a team of African American all-stars, college and professional. The game was to take place on September 23, 1938. (Back then, NFL seasons often had interruptions. By then, Halas' Bears had already played two league games, but they had two free weeks late that month.) Various Chicago charities were to share in the game's proceeds. Hull House, the Abraham Lincoln Center, and the Central District of the United Charities of Chicago were to divide 50 percent of the net proceeds. The players were to be paid $100 plus traveling expenses. Ozzie Simmons and Joe Lillard eagerly agreed to play. Other players from the minor professional circuits and from the neglected African American college teams turned out as well. Ray Kemp and Duke Slater served as coaches.

The all-stars' game preparations were unfortunately hasty and haphazard. Meanwhile, the Bears were in full season form, having already completed summer practice, pre-season games, and two regular season games. They were also rested and injury free. Practice for the African American all-stars was supposed to begin September 6, but it did not begin until September 9. Some of the players did not arrive until the game was but a week away; a few came with even shorter notice. Iowa's Homer Harris arrived but one day before the game. Coaches Kemp and Slater could have refused any late-comers, but if they determined the particular players to be valuable, there was nothing they could do about lateness besides vent a meaningless scolding. During practice, not everyone had proper equipment and shoes. Amidst the talk during the days of preparation, players began to grumble among one another, spreading fears that they were not going to receive their traveling reimbursements or their $100. Players did have to earn a spot on the team to be paid. Amidst preparations, Kemp brought in two players from Lincoln University (of Pennsylvania) where he coached. This caused further grumbling, as the two appeared clearly to have guaranteed spots on the team. In such an atmosphere, elements of fear and paranoia will easily grow, and any rumor will be believed. The rumors about no travel money or salaries were untrue, but Coach Kemp never addressed the matters during practices. He spoke reassuringly to the team about finances, but only minutes before the game. If Kemp was intentionally holding back on the facts about money so he could spring the truth on everyone to motivate them just prior to the game, he greatly miscalculated. The climate of suspicion hurt the team's morale as well as its preparations.[10]

While players like Simmons and Lillard could run with any NFL player, no running back can achieve success without good line play in front of him, and Kemp's team just could not produce at the line against the Bears. They were much lighter than their opponents, and the lack of quality practice was pivotal. Whatever such explanations, and whatever the issues of practice, personnel, and pay, the Bears won in a complete rout, 51–0. Their total offense was over 600 yards, and they were forced to punt only once in the entire game. Covering the game, the conservative *Chicago Tribune* chortled sarcastically, "The outstanding colored football players in the United States, selected in a nation-wide poll, held the Chicago Bears to 7 touchdowns, a field goal, and 6 extra points." William Nunn of the *Pittsburgh Courier* lamented that the lopsided loss would set the prospects of African Americans' advancement in sports like football back many years.[11]

Despite the lopsided score, Bears' coaches could still see individuals of talent on Kemp's squad, but no one was offered a professional contract. Lillard, Simmons, and other talented players had to continue to labor in the obscurity of pro football's minor leagues.

The career of Kenneth Washington, while it would later mark the eventual integration of the NFL, was for the most part yet another example, like that of Ozzie Simmons and Wilmeth Sidat-Singh, of how undeniably visible talent was allowed to go untapped because of racism. In the late 1930s, Washington was one of, if not *the* top col-

lege football players in the nation. He starred at UCLA from 1937 to
1939. Like Joe Lillard, Washington could do everything (although he
did not punt). Washington was one of the greatest "outside" speed
backs of the day. He was a great pass receiver, and he could throw the
ball farther than anyone in the game. One pass he completed flew 72
yards, the longest ariel completion any game, college or pro, had then
ever recorded. In 1939 Washington was named to many All-America
polls. In several cases he was a consensus choice. Still, as the 1940 season approached, no NFL team had offered Washington so much as a
try out, despite their giving opportunities to scores of lesser players.
Washington was nevertheless invited to play in Chicago's College All-
Star game against the NFL's defending champions, Green Bay. Washington was one of the few uncontracted players on the all-star squad,
and no one could miss the conspicuousness of this. The Packers won
the game, but Washington played well, both running and throwing.
After the game, with no team to which to return, Washington remained
in Chicago for a week, apparently at the private request of George
Halas. That week, Washington played for a minor league team while
Halas was likely telephoning various NFL owners, asking their
approval to bring this multi-talented player into the league. Result: at
the end of the week, Washington headed back to Los Angeles. The
owners would not budge about the color line they had drawn in 1933.
Halas would ask, but he would not press the point. Washington would
have been quite an addition to the 1940 Bears team that would win
the NFL championship that fall anyway and earn the nickname "the
Monsters of the Midway."

For the ensuing seasons during the World War II years, Washington played in the obscurity of the Pacific Coast Football Conference for a minor league team called the Hollywood Bears. His coach,
Paul Schlissler, the same Schlissler who had coached Joe Lillard in
Chicago, called Washington "the greatest all around player I have ever
coached or seen." While Washington certainly played well for the
Bears, it was clearly a waste, and in more ways than one. He should
have been playing for the Chicago Bears; in California the excellence
was visible only to a few. Beyond this, while playing minor league
football, Washington incurred several serious injuries to his knees. So
by 1946, when the newly relocated Los Angeles Rams signed the then
28-year-old Kenneth Washington and re-broke the color line in the
NFL, they had a player who had then undergone two serious knee
operations (with pre-arthroscopic knee operations being vastly more
traumatic), and who had lost much of his fabulous speed and cutting
ability. Washington would be the one to break the color line, but he

did it with little pizzazz and with the tragic knowledge that six years before he could have easily been one of the game's major stars.

Two of Washington's UCLA teammates also had bona fide professional credentials. Woodrow Strode was one. He too was never given an opportunity to play in the NFL until he was much older. The other UCLA great of those pre–World War II days was Jackie Robinson, who was one year behind Washington and Strode. Robinson too could have played in the NFL. He, of course, would break other ground.

Eight

Trials of the War Years

Considering what occurred between the NFL's refusing such a talent as Kenneth Washington in 1940 and their acceptance of him and other African American players starting in 1946, one must consider more broadly what happened to many of the nation's sensibilities during the years of World War II, for the nation underwent a significant social transformation, one that permanently shook the foundations of Jim Crow. When the Congress declared war in December 1941, much of the nation was already primed to take up the cause against the Japanese, the Nazis, and their allies. This was different than in World War I; in 1941 there was virtually no haziness in most Americans' minds as to who the demons were in the conflict. Isolationists could not put any sort of positive face on the policies and atrocities of the Axis powers; few ever attempted to do so. Most who had been isolationists before Pearl Harbor, like aviator Charles Lindbergh, jumped into line with the U.S. entry into the war.

Much the same pattern of sensibilities and expressions existed in African American communities. From 1939 to 1941, some African American organizations and many activists, notably W.E.B. Dubois, had stood in opposition to America's possible entry into the war. Editorials in the *Chicago Defender* and the *Pittsburgh Courier* also printed various isolationist views. The isolationism among African Americans was reinforced by the sense of the priorities with respect to political and social injustices to be fought. Editorialists for the *Defender* and the *Courier* raised points that the greater fight for African Americans was with Nazi-type oppression closer to home. "Our war is not against Hitler in Europe," wrote the *Courier*'s columnist George Schuyler, "but against the Hitlers in America."

Some tiny cults and radical groups of this era, like the Brotherhood of Liberty for Black People of America, the Ethiopian Pacific Movement, and the World Wide Friends of Africa, also voiced opposition to America's involvement in the war before Pearl Harbor. Some of those involved here had written and orated about the need for the darker-skinned people of the world to unite against their light-skinned oppressors. They saw the continued worldwide colonialism of nations like the United States, France, and Great Britain to be more their fight than the one between Adolph Hitler and Winston Churchill. In this racial context a few of these radical African American groups regarded the Japanese as allies in the fight of darker skinned people against white supremacy.

While such views dotted the landscape of African American perspectives, they were still exceedingly rare in the mainstream of African American communities. The average African American was vehemently anti-fascist. When Mussolini invaded Ethiopia in 1936, African American communities were indeed among the most vocal in the nation's protest. In several cities, notably in New York, clashes broke out between African American and nearby Italian neighborhoods, with many Italian Americans still feeling positively about Mussolini in the years before he allied himself with Hitler.*

While the African American communities stood overwhelmingly with mainstream America in support of the war, the obvious ironies of a Jim Crow nation standing in opposition to Hitler's racial doctrines was too obvious to ignore. And the answer for many patriotic African Americans was not to ignore it but to use it, as the *Pittsburgh Courier* suggested, "to persuade, embarrass, compel and shame our government and our nation ... into a more enlightened attitude toward a tenth of its people."

Amidst the clear ideological contradictions between anti–Hitler propaganda and the maintenance of Jim Crow, various African American leaders began to lobby for African Americans to share in both the burdens and the economic gains of the war years. When Nazi prisoners of war were transported to Southern camps, and the railroads crossed into such states as Kentucky and Virginia, African American

---

Sports played a role in these Italian–African American clashes, as in June 1935, exactly a year prior to Mussolini's incursion into Ethiopia, nasty conflicts between Italians and blacks erupted when boxer Joe Louis soundly defeated the bumbling, mafia-owned Italian heavyweight Primo Carnera. During the weeks of hype that preceded the Louis-Carnera fight, Mussolini was already behaving belligerently and orating pompously in regard to Ethiopia. A year later, Italian Americans then celebrated Mussolini's slaughter of Ethiopians in front of many African Americans with an added factor of revenge for their humiliation over Carnera's embarrassingly feeble performance against Louis. The resulting clashes between Italians and blacks were indeed highly charged affairs.

soldiers assigned to guard the prisoners had to yield their railroad seats, not just to white American travelers but to the German POWs as well. In the armed services, African American men were susceptible to the military draft, just like whites, yet they were relegated to segregated units. The Army Air Corps and the Marines had a simple "no blacks" rule of enlistment. The Navy accepted African Americans but assigned them almost exclusively to food operations. The Army maintained racially separate units, with circumscribed "appropriate" duties like supply, maintenance, and food service being the norms. The American Red Cross actually refused to accept blood from African Americans who wanted to donate, even during such critical times as late 1944 when American casualties were mounting and plasma supplies were running perilously low. An added irony here was the fact that the technique of spinning blood into storable plasma was perfected by an African American physician, Dr. Charles Drew, although the infamous story that Dr. Drew bled to death after a white-only hospital emergency room refused him when he arrived there after an auto accident is not true. Dr. Drew's daughter has always confirmed this. The false story has been told again and again. Among its many renditions, it appeared in the politically earnest '70s TV show *M*A*S*H* and has remained a canard ever since.[1] The famous Dr. Drew was, truthfully, the same Charles Drew who played football for Amherst from 1923 to 1925.

The embarrassing ironies and hypocrisies of American laws, customs, and policies created a backdrop for some effective lobbying by several African American leaders. Most noteworthy here was the work of A. Philip Randolph, head of the Brotherhood of Sleeping Car Porters labor union. Incensed particularly by segregation in the armed forces and in the growing armaments industries, Randolph resolved to organize a protest march of African Americans in Washington, D.C., in the summer of 1941. (The war had not begun for the United States, but armament industries were already growing with Lend Lease; the draft was fully in effect; and every person with a shred of political acumen knew the propaganda value that a march of African Americans would have for Nazis and their friends against the self-proclaimed "Arsenal of Democracy.") Randolph's effort was called the MOWM, the March on Washington Movement.

Randolph grasped the point that any mass protest against such a problem as racism in America would be a potential embarrassment the Roosevelt administration would seek to avoid at almost any cost. Randolph proved quite perceptive. For several months he wrote Roosevelt, cagily telling him of the numbers of people who planned to attend the rally. 50,000, 75,000, 100,000, the numbers kept climbing. Roosevelt invited Randolph to a meeting at the White House to try to work out the problem before any such embarrassing march took place. Roosevelt tried to win Randolph over with his infamous charm, but at the meeting Randolph was blunt with the President about the indignities African Americans were continuing to endure. To this Roosevelt ultimately made several promises. One promise actually proved to be a flat-out lie—that the President would move to integrate the nation's armed forces. Roosevelt never even attempted to institute this. (Harry Truman once conceded that a major problem with FDR was that he would indeed quite readily lie.) Randolph would be outraged here, but other Roosevelt promises did materialize to some degree. Roosevelt agreed to issue Executive Orders, the first prohibiting racial or religious discrimination in the defense industries, and the second creating a Committee on Fair Employment Practices.

During Lend Lease, and even more after Pearl Harbor, while receiving fat "cost plus" contracts from the War Department, many industries had been adamant in their refusals to hire African Americans. With ungrammatical obnoxiousness, for example, North American Aviation sniffed: "The Negro will be considered only as janitors and in other similar capacities. Regardless of their training as aircraft workers, we will not employ them." The aircraft industry's workforce at the beginning of the war was ¼ percent black. Simultaneously, the electrical industry's was but one percent; the rubber industry's was just under three percent. Roosevelt promised that industries would be pressured by the Federal government to change their employment practices, and to stop their non-hiring practices and their relegation of African Americans to low-level, low-pay jobs.

Randolph agreed to call off the march. MOWM activities and the jobs that began to come to African Americans during the war nevertheless helped begin a major change of political mood in the country. While some political leaders had been active and militant in regard to the many social, economic, and political issues of African Americans for many years, with the jobs and opportunities of the war years there developed among the masses of African Americans a new hope and a quiet resolve that the old ways were simply not going to continue. Militancy and activism among what W.E.B. DuBois had freely described as "the talented tenth" of African Americans may have been necessary in prior eras of extreme repression and violence. World War II created a situation in which massive grass roots levels of hope replaced older norms of militancy among a few, and of begrudging complacency or despair among many. Voices for activism no longer had to confront the vast levels of fear that dominated in regions which had afforded no opportunities for economic advancement. By 1945, nearly 3/4 million African Americans served in the armed forces during the war. Millions had decently paying jobs. Life had changed for far too many people; the institutional arrangements of the nation had gone through too many adjustments; and too many African Americans risked their lives fighting racism abroad for old Jim Crow ways ever to come back unchallenged.

Whenever such administrative changes as the Roosevelt administration began are to be instituted, the devil lies in the details. Here such obstacles as those of entrenched Jim Crow traditions were enormous. An African American member of Congress, Arthur Mitchell, for example, was ordered to vacate a Pullman berth while traveling by rail in Arkansas.[2] The levels of enforced segregation among troops sent to training bases in the South was a shock, even to many white soldiers from Northern and Western states. (With African Americans having to give up rail seats to German POWs, shock turned into utter consternation, at least among a few.) Given the context of the nation fighting for the cause of stopping the Nazis' racism, this was all so obviously ironic. Especially surprising here was the level of apartheid that sprang forth the moment any soldier stepped off the grounds of Southern military bases. The massive number of Northerners who witnessed this during the war would provide a further backdrop for the changes that would come to America after the war, as the common pre-war out-of-sight, out-of-mind outlook about Jim Crow among many Northern whites could not so easily continue; too much had become known.

In such a state of affairs, some of FDR's chief subordinates still did little other than drag their feet in regard to race questions. Roosevelt's elderly Secretary of War, Henry L. Stimson, for example, complained about "these foolish leaders of the colored race ... seeking social equality." J. Edgar Hoover continued to disallow any African Americans from attaining agent status in the FBI. Others in the Roosevelt administration were more forthright, however. Here one of the unsung heroes in the history of the erosion of Jim Crow during World War II was FDR's Navy Secretary, James N. Forrestall. Led by Forrestall's particularly conscientious work, the navy moved toward integration. Some Southern commanders at bases in Great Britain were disciplined, and in a few cases relieved of duty, for trying to institute segregation practices. Due to Forrestall, as well as to others, armament industries also felt pressure to change their employment practices. The high demand for employees was also forcing these industries to seek labor wherever they could get it. (Unlike the older slavery days, the impetus for productivity and, hence, for economic logic, came from the outside; parochial cultural ways thus could not be so illogically subverting and indulgent of poor productivity, as they had been in the ante-bellum era. World War II could simply not accommodate the economic costs of Jim Crow.) Between 1942 and 1945, African American employment in the armament industries rose from roughly three percent to eight percent, a level nearly at parity with respect to African Americans' percentage in the nation's overall population.

Where jobs for African Americans grew, some tensions emerged, as had occurred during World War I. A series of particularly nasty racial conflicts broke out in Detroit in June 1943, for example. Other such incidents occurred elsewhere, as wartime necessities compelled levels of integration and exchange between races in housing and job areas. Hispanics encountered much the same hostility and occasions of violence in the Southwest during the war years too. In other instances, though, the changes were positive. While it did not make the newspapers or the police records, in millions of cases the years of the war saw blacks and whites working alongside one another and discovering that it was no big deal. When boxer Joe Louis was drafted, the army, somewhat shamefully many thought, used him on their recruiting posters, in scores of boxing exhibitions, and in a propaganda film, *The Negro Soldier*. Louis was asked how he felt about such work, particularly the fighting of all those boxing exhibitions for nothing. His famous response was: "I'm not fighting for nothing, I'm fighting for my country.... I'm only doing what any red-blooded American would do." Such blunt words gained the admiration of many, black and white, and diffused many tensions and points of militancy and resistance. The Red Cross did not pay sufficient heed of Louis' comment, however, and continued to reject African American blood donations. While there was an enormous legacy to overcome, American society was nevertheless beginning to change.

Nine

The Early Saga of Marion Motley

The life of Marion Motley, who would be one of the four players to integrate professional football in 1946, embodied many of the dynamics of the entrenched old and emerging new ways that flitted about the pathways of American culture in the years leading up to World War II, as well as during the war and after. Motley was born to a poor farm family in Georgia. The life of his family in the 1920s was no different than that which millions of black sharecroppers had endured since Reconstruction. There was only the prospect of a life of poverty, surrounded by the potentials of terror and violence, especially if someone dared to challenge the political status quo. Like many African American families in the 1920s, in hopes of a better life for their children, the Motleys moved north. They settled in Massillon, Ohio, where Marion Motley's father found a decently paying job in one of the local steel mills. It was in Massillon that Marion Motley went to high school and first played organized football. There his athletic talents came forth in abundance.

As it had been in the early twentieth century, football continued to be a religion to folks in the mill towns of Eastern Ohio, and by the 1930s, with the "matured" NFL having eclipsed the small Ohio communities which had been some of the league's early mainstays, these towns turned ever more to high school football as the focus of their local pride and sports fanaticism. Among Massillon's fans, the big football rival continued to be nearby Canton. While there was no longer an annual Massillon-Canton professional football war, the Massillon-Canton High School football game was a November occasion of enormous importance for all football fans in Eastern Ohio. Motley played for Massillon from 1937 to 1939, and during those years Canton was one of the state's top teams, quite possibly the best high school team in the nation. Meanwhile, the Massillon team was the only school in the region that could begin to rival Canton. Canton was led by an exacting young coach named Paul Brown. Under Brown, Canton's teams had a five-year record of 59 and 1. The lone defeat came in the final game of 1939. This was against Massillon, and in that game Marion Motley almost singlehandedly ran and tackled Canton into submission. (Like most players of the era, Motley played "both ways," and was the best both at fullback and at linebacker.) Paul Brown would not forget the huge Massillon player who had so soundly defeated him.

With the ongoing racial prejudice of the era, Motley had few offers to play college football, though many demonstrably lesser white players of his team did. There is no way that Ohio State or other Big Ten teams could not have been aware of Motley. Nevertheless, he could only accept admission to a segregated Southern school—South Carolina State A and T in Orangeburg, South Carolina. Why Motley first chose to attend school in the South he never fully explained. Perhaps he felt a certain nostalgia for a region he had only known as a small boy; perhaps he did not like the weather in Ohio. Perhaps he just had a youthful curiosity about some place far away. Whatever his reasoning, the choice proved not to be a happy one for him. He played a season in Orangeburg, but he was not content with the utterly ensconced Jim Crow ways of late '30s South Carolina. He played well and received a little good press. Papers were uniform in their praise of Motley as a "hard driving fullback." Generally, though, Motley played in relative obscurity, as local newspapers gave little coverage to "colored schools." The region was certainly not to his liking. Local papers were then gleefully bragging about how the Ku Klux Klan was increasing in membership—"KKK to Ride Again" headlined Columbia, South Carolina's paper. The reporting was done with the apparent intention of smugly warning any who sought or even thought about social change.[1]

Whatever boyhood nostalgia Motley may have held for the region, it seemed quickly to vanish as he felt the sting of the segregation customs of Western South Carolina, a region with as high a degree of unreconstructed Jim Crowism as anywhere in the nation. After the football season and the first semester of classes were over, Motley left. Perhaps still wanting a warm climate, perhaps with a simple and natural desire to travel, the young Motley headed West. His high school coach, Jimmy Aiken, left Ohio to coach at the University of Nevada.[2] Motley then enrolled at the University of Nevada at Reno, where he would play football starting in the fall of 1940.

The racial attitudes in the West seemed looser and more mixed. There was prejudice to be sure, but even where it existed it was far less laced with the utterly ensconced Jim Crow practices of late '30s South Carolina. People at the University of Nevada seemed to take well to their new football star. Reporters certainly made explicit the fact that this football player was a "huge colored lad." Another nick-named him "the dark dynamiter," but there was admiration in the columns, and no deeply seeded segregationist customs about him. With plenty of praise for his football, all with good reason of course, Mot-ley seemed to be happy in Nevada.

On the Nevada team, Motley was doing everything. As a line-backer he was the team's lead tackler. He was doing the place kick-ing. He was throwing many of the offense's forward passes, and, naturally, he was the main running back. With Motley doing so much for them, the Nevada-Reno fans had high hopes for their "Wolf Pack," and Motley was touted as potential All-American material. The rest of the team, however, was not strong.[3]

The early part of the season went well for Motley and the Wolves. They won the first game against San Francisco State 47–0, and Mot-ley ran so well "that several times he dragged half the ... tacklers along with him several more feet." One reporter made a point of noting that the team had apparently no race issues. This revealed itself when sev-eral Nevada players moved in threateningly on one San Francisco player who had slugged Motley.

In a rain soaked game against Brigham Young, Motley could not run well amidst the muddy conditions. No one could, and the game ended in a dreary 6–6 tie. Motley was not faulted for once fumbling the wet ball, and his pile-driving running again drew praise, even among the reporters from Salt Lake City. "Fans like Motley," neatly noted a Reno reporter. After the Brigham Young tie, Nevada went on to crush several foes: Idaho Southern 62–0, Arkansas A and M 78–0, and Eastern New Mexico 40–6. Motley was averaging nearly 15 yards per carry. During the games various Southern players irked Motley with their verbal abuse and "extracurricular" piling on and gouging. This was part of the reason that the scores were so lopsided. Motley was riled at the racism. Key here was the fact that the team was com-pletely with him as they exacted revenge for the abuse of their star teammate.[4]

Motley appeared to have found a happy home in Nevada. He was playing superbly. The team was riding on his big back, and appar-ently he felt no racial pressure on the campus or among his team-mates. Then this happy new world came crashing down on him. While no reporter had discussed it beforehand, Motley had been involved in an automobile accident back in March of 1940. When Motley left South Carolina, he had immediately headed to Nevada. While in Reno, he and a friend were on a weekend trip to San Francisco; Motley was driving. He tried to pass a vehicle. The other motorist (his motive unknown) decided to increase his speed to prevent Motley from passing. Caught in the passing lane, Motley then collided with an oncoming car. Several people were injured in the crash, and one elderly man in the other car was seriously hurt. He died of pneumonia a few days later. While the issue of fault was debatable, on October 29, 1940, Marion Motley was convicted of negligent homicide.

Motley's conviction came just after the Eastern New Mexico game. Whether Motley had been able up to that point to put the matter out of his mind, or whether he was worrying about it throughout the months since the accident, playing football had certainly been a happy release from the issue. Now that was all snatched away from him. He could not play in the team's next game against Fresno State College. He had to leave Nevada and await his sentence in the Solano County, California, jail. The court judge, W.T. O'Daniel, made a statement to the press that there was but a "slight chance of probation."

Nevada reporters noted how hard the entire campus and community were taking the news of Motley's conviction. Indicative of how warmly the students and local football fans had taken to Motley, reporters went out of their way to counsel local fans not to attempt to induce the judge and jury to be lenient, as they could "resent pressure from over-zealous fans." "Remain hopeful but cool" was the advice. In the game against Fresno, Nevada lost 7–6; up to then, the Nevada paper pointed out, the team's point total against their combined opposition had been 233–12. To say the least, they missed Motley.[5]

With Motley in jail awaiting sentencing, Nevada students began a collection drive on his behalf. Newspapers wrote sympathetically of the precarious "future of a fine young gentleman, convicted of negligent homicide under circumstances that could involve you or me or anyone else." Precedent in both Nevada and California law indicated the possibility of $1000 fine and probation as a possible outcome, so the students sought to raise that very amount of money. Organizations and individuals stepped forward with donations. At the center of the Nevada campus quadrangle, students erected a "Fund Thermometer" with the $1000 goal at the top. Every day the red marker on the thermometer inched higher and higher, with donations from students, from merchants, and from classes of local elementary school students. It worked! They raised the full amount. Meanwhile, Judge O'Daniel indeed chose to fine Motley $1000 and sentence him to three years probation. He could spend the three years of probation on the Nevada campus, with a Nevada English professor, Paul Harwood, administering the probation. Marion Motley was again a free man.

A biting bit of irony in the story was that one of the inducements the thermometer leaders had publicized was the fact that the victim in the accident was Tom K. Nobori, "an aged Japanese." Racism against African Americans was indeed vastly less then in the West than in South Carolina. And certainly if the accident had occurred back in South Carolina and the victim had been white, Marion Motley would have likely gotten the death penalty or spent the rest of his life on a chain gang. In Nevada, Motley may have actually been helped by a different kind of prejudice that was most certainly on the rise in the West against the Japanese.

Returning to Nevada, Motley wrote a letter that appeared in the local paper, "To the students, faculty, and people of Nevada," he wrote humbly,

> while the service you rendered in my behalf was a complete surprise, it was very much appreciated. I cannot tell you in words how grateful I am for what you have done for me. I shall try to show it by the quality of the school work I do and the service I can render in behalf of the University of Nevada and the people of this state.[6]

Motley came back to play for Nevada for the rest of the season. The team suffered several key injuries, leading Motley ever more to shoulder the load. As a result, opposing teams could key completely on him. Nevada would lose the rest of their games. The media noted Motley's contributions, however, and he earned several reporters' All-American mentions.[7]

In Motley's next two seasons with Nevada, the saga was much the same. Opposing teams stationed one, sometimes even two defensive players exclusively to follow Motley. The Nevada team had no other significant talent. Against the University of San Francisco, Nevada was outweighed by an average of fifteen pounds per man, so the tactic of keying on Motley worked well. Media analysts recognized how good Motley was and lamented the waste of a player of his talent struggling with a team that could not support him. Motley also hurt his hip early in the 1941 season. Later that year he also hurt his ankle. Still, he kept playing. To ease the burden of running at linebacker on defense, Motley switched not off the defense but merely to the tackle position. Reporters here noted Motley's heart as well as his

Marion Motley. Having been a star at the University of Nevada (but never invited to play in the East-West Shrine Game), Motley appeared to be headed toward the same dead end that other African American college stars of the time faced. In 1946, however, the new Cleveland Browns signed Motley, and he became one of the greatest pro football running backs of all time.

ability.[8] Former University of California star Ernie Nevers wrote: "I'd like to see that fellow with two good legs under him. Motley is the fastest big man we've seen."[9]

Late in October 1941, Motley's troubles worsened. His hip and ankle were still bothering him; now he hurt his knee. Some days his knee was so swollen he could not practice. Still he played, breaking away on several exciting big gainers. Motley proved ever more that he not only had the ability but the fortitude to play football in any league. On November 13, one radio commentator named Motley the "All-American of the week." The San Francisco UPI named Motley as a potential All-American. Two days later, Motley ran for 116 yards in a game against California-Davis. When the season ended he was named to the All-Pacific Coast team.[10]

Motley's final season in Nevada in 1942 occurred, of course, with the nation at war. Manpower issues were already in evidence on many football teams. For Nevada this aggravated an already thin talent situation. In that season of 1942, Motley was the only back on the team who weighed more than 160 pounds! Even more than in the prior two seasons, Motley was a one-man team, and all his opponents again keyed on him. Southern recruits playing for the University of New Mexico made a special point of piling on and roughing up Motley whenever they could. Motley never retaliated, but his injured knee began to give him trouble again.[11]

While Motley encountered little racism on the Nevada campus, he would never escape it, and the words and dirty tactics of the New Mexico players were only one example. With the war, army-air bases were being established near Reno, and "Negro" troops were never allowed on them. General David Joyce, commanding general at Fort Douglas, Utah, went out of his way to promise the people of Reno: "it is not now contemplated that any colored troops be assigned to the vicinity.... In the event, however, that it becomes necessary to change the present plans in the region, you will be given advanced notice thereof if possible."[12]

The season wound down for the weak Nevada team. Their record was 4–2–1. With the end of the season Motley's eligibility had run out, and a bit sooner than he had a right to expect. For years the Shriners organization had staged a December all-star game of Eastern and Western college football players. With the proceeds going to war charities, the game was planned for December 1942 in San Francisco. For the second time, Motley had been named to UPI's All-American list; this time it was almost unanimous. He was also named to several All-Pacific squads. The Shriners had already refused to let UCLA's Kenny Washington play in their charity game in 1939. In 1942 they chose to overlook Marion Motley too. There was only one explanation.[13]

The Nevada newspapers noted the snub of their star, and that was certainly indicative of some of the sympathy that contrasted to the utterly entrenched racism Motley saw back in South Carolina. But with the behavior of the Shriners, with the specter of Kenny Washington laboring nearby in obscurity and for little pay with the Hollywood Bears, and with the adamant color bar of the NFL, Motley could only conclude that the University of Nevada-Reno marked the end of the line for his football career. With no prospects, Motley, bum knee and all, went back to Ohio and took a job in a foundry with Republic Steel. Though it appeared to mark the end of his sports career, there were several good things about the move. For one thing, the foundry was a steady, well-paying job. Additionally, as Motley later reflected, the incessant heat in the foundry had a wonderfully salubrious effect on his troubled knee.

After a year at the foundry, a now healthy Motley joined the Navy in late 1944. The war in Europe ended as Motley's training was taking place. Anticipating more years of war with Japan (before knowledge of the atom bomb), the armed services did not immediately close down bases. Even after Japan's surrender, bases were phased out gradually. The base to which Motley had been assigned—the Great Lakes Naval Training Station outside Chicago—was not slated to close until 1946. As it had during World War I, Great Lakes was blessed with some strong athletic talent and boasted a fine football team. Army and Navy officials were often able to influence the troop assignments so they could bolster their bases' athletic rosters, and there is no question that Motley's fame as a football player led to his assignment to Great Lakes. The Great Lakes Station also had a baseball team with such players as Schoolboy Rowe, Mickey Cochrane, Pinky Higgins, and Bob Feller. Even with the war over, Great Lakes continued to play football in the fall of 1945.

During Motley's college career, Paul Brown had left his coaching post at Canton and taken the head coaching job at Ohio State University. After the 1943 season, he enlisted in the Navy. Lieutenant Paul Brown was assigned to Great Lakes, where he coached the Station's team. (Base commanders knew how to pick coaches as well as athletes.) It was at Great Lakes that Paul Brown first linked up with Motley since the Massillon—Canton game of 1939. In the summer of 1945, with the Great Lakes Training Station slated for a phase out, bases on the West Coast were being expanded in anticipation of the continuing war with Japan. Base commanders in California were able to expand their personnel, and the commanders, like those at Great Lakes, had eyes on good camp sports teams and knew where to look for talent among the ranks—Great Lakes. The commander of the Fleet City Base near San Francisco was particularly adept at securing athletic talent. "By some means which I never did understand," recalled Paul Brown, "our players were transferred one by one to Fleet City."

From his excellent 1944 squad, Paul Brown lost several prominent players who would later play in the NFL—Eddie Saenz and Jim Youell of the Washington Redskins, George Young of the Cleveland Browns, Jim Keane of the Chicago Bears, as well as Ara Parseghian who would later coach Notre Dame. They all went to the Fleet City Base. Brown was able to hold onto Marion Motley, however. At that point, Brown believed, Motley was still a relative unknown. Brown may have been kind to his Naval brethren here, as race may have played a key role in the choice not to transfer Motley. Brown claimed that Motley "had not been at the University of Nevada long enough to build a great reputation," but Motley had been there for three full seasons, and the West Coast papers had given him plenty of coverage.[14]

James Forrestall had wanted integration to grow in the Navy, and Brown was never one to care about a player's race. While at Ohio State, Brown had outraged some Ohioans of Southern sensibility with his non-segregation attitude; Brown was never one to pay heed to pressure that did not make intrinsic sense with respect to the athletic tasks before him. If a player could do the job for him, that was all Paul Brown needed to know. Race was simply not an issue. With Brown's success at Ohio State, racist Ohioans could only mutter and grouse quietly. At Ohio State, one of Brown's best defensive linemen, for example, was Bill Willis, the first African American to star at football and earn All-America status for the university.

At Great Lakes, Brown knew he had a winner in Marion Motley, and after three seasons with a weak team in Nevada, Motley relished playing with such an aggregate of quality players, as well as with a coach like Paul Brown. At first things were a little rocky, however. One of the problems of the sports teams of the nation's many military bases was the fact that they had huge turnover in personnel year to year and had little pre-season practice time. In September of 1945, Brown had 300 Naval personnel try out for his football team. He had them down to 50 in a week.

One of the 50 was an eighteen year old named Harry "Bud" Grant from Superior, Wisconsin, later the coach of the Minnesota Vikings. Grant recalled his first encounter with Marion Motley: "There was this big black fellow," Grant later recalled, "who I had a very tough time tackling, and I became very interested in what he was going to play when [Coach Brown] finally called us by position. I watched him go over to where the rest of the fullbacks were, and at that moment I became an end, because there was no way I was going to beat Marion Motley. I didn't know him and hadn't heard of him, but I knew he was awfully tough."[15]

As a result of Service duties getting in the way of practice, and the hurried assemblage of a Base team in the pre-season, the best way to beat many of the Army and Naval Base teams was to play them early in the season. From mid-season on, given their experience, their age (usually a few years more advanced than that of their college opponents), and their steadily improving teamwork, especially with a man like Paul Brown coaching, they would be fearsome. Great Lakes would show this pattern.

At the beginning of the season Great Lakes lost to the University of Michigan. Having practiced with the team only a little, Motley did not play well. Papers noted that Motley appeared "unseasoned," but they praised the "gigantic Negro fullback," noting he put "a big scare into Michigan."[16] Motley had Navy duties that kept him from playing in Great Lakes' next two games, which ended in a 0–0 tie with Wisconsin and a 20–6 loss to Purdue. Then the team had two weeks off, during which they practiced and had Marion Motley's services full time. As a result, Motley led Great Lakes to finish the season with a run of six straight victories over Marquette, Western Michigan, Illinois, Michigan State, Fort Warren (Wyoming), and, in their big finale, over Notre Dame. Motley was the star of all the victories. Against Illinois he ran a kickoff back 73 yards.

Before the Notre Dame game Motley and another player were actually eligible for discharge. Brown announced to them before a practice: "I've been notified that you have finished your tour and may leave. Or I can arrange to delay your discharge until after we play Notre Dame. Which will it be?" Brown recalled at that point the players "looked at me with a bit of steel in their eyes, and [one player] said with a big grin on his face, 'Coach, we've gone this far, and I don't think the extra ten bucks the Navy has to pay us is going to bust the government.' Motley nodded his approval."[17] Against Notre Dame, the *Chicago Tribune* reported that Motley "advanced at will." One run went for 44 yards.[18] Great Lakes' victory over Notre Dame was especially sweet. Paul Brown counted it among the six greatest thrills of his football career. It was the final game of the season. Notre Dame had been highly touted all year. The Naval Station was already slated for dismantling, so this would be their last game ever. As Great Lakes would no longer exist, their victory over Notre Dame, combined with previous victories during World War I and World War II, gave the team a permanent won-loss edge over the fabled Irish, the only team to have this distinction (save for tiny Knox College of Galesburg, Illinois, who played and beat Notre Dame once).

The season with the Great Lakes Station was a bonus for Motley, but when it was over it again looked like the end of his football playing. Motley was discharged from the Navy, and he went back to Ohio, where a wife and three children waited for him to get a job and support them.

Three months after Motley's departure, Paul Brown also received his discharge papers from the Navy. He had been the coach at Ohio State through the 1943 season. Then came his stint with the Navy. With Brown's departure, and with the drafting and volunteering of so many young men into the service, Ohio State athletic officials figured the 1944 season would be a waste. But before the '44 season, the Army and the War Department reversed their prior position of not allowing students in ROTC to play sports. As a result, Ohio State fielded a great team and went undefeated in 1944. Ohio State's Athletic Director, Lynn St. John, had previously promised Paul Brown that he could have his job back when he completed his commitments with the Navy. Both St. John and Brown had anticipated this would be a welcome reunion, but after the surprising season of 1944, St. John suddenly conveyed a markedly different tone: "We made an agreement, and we'll live by it," Brown recalled St. John telling him. "You're welcome to return ... but you must know it may be a bit sticky after [Interim Coach Carroll] Widdoes's unbeaten season." Brown later confessed: "I needed more than that."[19] So as the spring of 1946 approached, Marion Motley and Paul Brown were each looking for work.

Ten

The Walls Come Tumbling Down

At the beginning of 1946, a proven football star who happened to be black, like Marion Motley, appeared to have in store for him the same fate as had befallen Wilmeth Sidat-Singh, Brud Holland, and Ozzie Simmons—absolutely no chance to play for the major professional football teams. Marion Motley and Kenneth Washington happened to live at a precipitous time, however. The war had changed much in the nation. Many people had come to a recognition that if individuals of different races could work together in a monumental enterprise like the war effort, they could do so as well in such comparatively insignificant operations as those of sports teams. To be sure, there were still going to be major levels of resistance to any major social changes. But at the very least, the racist forces of complacency no longer held the field unchallenged.

Upon the end of the war, with some hopes for a growing economy, an enterprising spirit caught the fancy of many who felt the new post-war era could enliven wider markets for spectators/consumers in various forms of entertainment, including sports. In the sports businesses there grew desires to expand. Boxing promoters found renewed interest in the fight game, and fight cards drew large paying crowds all over the nation. Within a year of the end of the war, a new professional league began in basketball—the National Basketball Association. (Like Major League Baseball and the NFL, the NBA was racially segregated in its first years, and in 1946 the NBA champion Minneapolis Lakers lost a post-season game to the Harlem Globetrotters. Still, NBA owners did not relent with regard to black players for another four years, and then the changes were painfully slow.)

Certain new "sports" like roller derby and professional wrestling began to expand. Baseball first remained steady, however, with its ongoing eight-team, all-white American and National Leagues and parallel black leagues, and with the disbanding of such interim innovations of the war years as a women's league. There was, however, an unsuccessful attempt at starting a rival baseball league in Mexico, one that was fielding racially integrated teams. (An attempt by one representative of the Mexican League to recruit Josh Gibson from Pittsburgh led the rep. finding himself unceremoniously dumped out of Forbes Field and onto the streets of Pittsburgh.)[1] Geographic expansion would not come to baseball until 1953 when the Braves left Boston for Milwaukee. Other moves, such as the Dodgers' infamous move to Los Angeles, would follow. The expansion in the number of major league teams would not come until 1962.

Football was the game that showed the professional sports world's first major changes. The Cleveland Rams had been the NFL champions in 1945. At the end of the season, the Rams' owners decided to become the first major American sports organization to resettle on the Pacific coast and tap the burgeoning Western market. The Rams moved to Los Angeles. Meanwhile, a group of businessmen in eight cities decided to form a second professional football league. They called their organization the All-American Football Conference.*

Like most fledgling sports conferences, the AAFC was somewhat haphazard in organization during its early days. Some teams, like the Cleveland Browns and the San Francisco 49'ers, were well financed and professionally run. Others, like the Miami Seahawks and the Buffalo Bisons, were rather marginal outfits. Cleveland's coach, Paul Brown, recalled how the Miami team owner seemed way out of his element when dealing with the rest of the conference team owners. (He could not even comfortably play poker with them.) While playing road games in 1946, the Miami team sometimes left town without paying their hotel bills, forcing the rest of the league to cover the debts.[2] Like their NFL counterparts, the AAFC owners had an informal accord not allowing African American players into the new league. The addition of the Miami team, the last of the eight teams to form, appeared to confirm this, and prominent African-American sports columnist Wendell Smith openly lamented this point, for the city of Miami and the state of Florida had laws forbidding racial mixing in athletic competition: "Any hopes football fans may have had for Negro

---

*The original eight teams were the New York Yankees, the Brooklyn Dodgers, the Buffalo Bisons, the Miami Seahawks, the Cleveland Browns, the San Francisco 49ers, the Los Angeles Dons, and the Chicago Rockets.

players in the All American Conference ... died recently when a franchise was awarded to a syndicate in Miami."[3]

Wendell Smith's anger and fears were certainly well founded, but in the fledgling AAFC, as was the case in the NFL in the 1920s, enforcement of any sort of gentlemen's agreement was going to be difficult. Cleveland coach Paul Brown, furthermore, was not someone who would follow any rules that did not make inherent sense to him. Brown had seen African American players when he coached at Canton High School, at Ohio State, and at the Great Lakes Naval Training Station. Brown was a meticulous individual who, in his desire to bring the game of football to a more precise scientific level, cared little about the pigment of a man's skin. He cared largely about how well a man could perform in the severe physical, mental, and personal tasks that he demanded. Here Brown was as tough (some would say at times peculiar) a stickler for detail as any coach in any sport. It was Brown who began mathematical measures of players, timing his players' 40-yard sprints, for example, the distance of a typical punt (hence a far more useful measure than any such track event as the 100-yard dash). He held classroom-type meetings to go over plays and strategy which many players likened to the toughest courses they took in college (and they took tough courses back then). Brown expected all players to take notes. He collected the notebooks and reviewed them; and he actually cut some players for poorly kept notebooks. On another occasion, when a player with a laudable college football record arrived at Brown's office door, knocked, and coarsely asked: "You Brown?" Brown took one look at the player's dirty pants and unshaven face and tersely responded: "Oh yes. I'm sorry, but there's been a mistake. The business manager will see that you get transportation home."[4] Amidst such meticulous concerns for detail, the matter of a man's race made little difference. Any who could excel within his rigid system were welcome.

It was in the summer of 1946, when training the new Cleveland team, that Brown brought into camp two African American players, both of whom would star and subsequently gain entry into the professional football Hall of Fame—Bill Willis and Marion Motley. Covering the Cleveland's new team, the *Cleveland Plain Dealer,* having taken little notice of Willis, who arrived first, noted the arrival of Motley with some sense of shock:

> The Browns revealed today that they have added a second great Negro player for a tryout in professional ranks. The newcomer is Marion Motley, a giant fullback who lives in Canton and was a star with Coach Paul Brown's Great Lakes Naval Training Station Team.

> Motley, who weighs around 225 pounds, made a surprise entry
> here this afternoon, and immediately was given a uniform and went
> through the Browns' workout....
> "He can play a game tomorrow," said Brown after the squad had
> left the field.
> Ten days ago, Coach Brown popped his first surprise when Bill
> Willis, former all-American tackle from Ohio State came here for a
> tryout.[5]

Bill Willis had played for Paul Brown at Ohio State. Willis was
a defensive lineman, and he was the kind of lineman that Brown liked—
quick and smart. Brown once reflected: "There's no place on my team
for Big Butch who talks hard and drinks hard. I like a lean and hun-
gry look."[6] Willis was one of the first players who saw the wisdom in
studying the minor habits and tendencies of the opposing center. He
would pay particular attention to the center's hands and fingers. Virtually every center against whom he played (as well as those with
whom he played in practice) had a pattern or habit which involved
some sort of hand or finger movement in the split seconds before he
snapped the ball to the quarterback or the kick holder. Willis would
quietly study and familiarize himself with these little patterns and thus
be able to begin his defensive charge at the earliest possible moment,
with and not after the snap of the ball. He was almost offsides on virtually every play. There were many times that Willis was able to get
past the offensive lineman opposite him before the man had been able
to take his blocking stance. He tackled many quarterbacks as they
were taking their first steps back to pass. And he tackled many runners at the moment they were taking a handoff. He did all these things
early in the Browns' training camp, and Coach Brown certainly noticed
it. Any Cleveland players who harbored hostilities about Willis having a chance to make the team had to acknowledge the man's talent.
Brown was direct here:

> I never considered football players black or white, nor did I keep or
> cut a player just because of his color. In our first meeting before train-
> ing camp every year, I told the players that they made our teams only
> if they were good enough.[7]

Although the Cleveland newspapers had taken little notice of Brown
bringing Willis into camp, with the addition of Motley it was clear
that the coach was serious about ignoring the customs of segregation.
Some said that the addition of Motley satisfied the sticky question of
road trip roommates; although Brown could have paid no heed to
such trivialities too.

In the manner in which Brown integrated the team, he may have actually been showing an astute regard for the political realities that were at play here. Outwardly, Brown always appeared to contend with any political consideration only in regard to what would be best for his professional goal—winning football games. But Brown certainly knew what was occurring beyond his little football camp in Bowling Green, Ohio. In the summer of 1946, when Brown was running his training camp, the sports world was already aflutter over baseball's Brooklyn Dodgers' signing of Jackie Robinson. (They signed him in March of 1946 with the intention of him playing for a season with their top minor league team in Montreal before elevating him to the major leagues.) Brown always claimed that he had wanted both Willis and Motley well before the day Branch Rickey signed Jackie Robinson, and had been thinking about how to go about bringing the two players into professional football with a minimum of public scrutiny and press coverage:

> Even though our sport did not have the same national impact as major league baseball at the time, I knew the fierce attention we would receive would create some unfair pressure which would in turn harm both players. I wanted to avoid that dangerous ground, so, to soften the impact as much as I could, I decided to wait until our team was settled into training camp before asking them to join us.... I think the delicate way in which we did it helped both of them to escape the tremendous pressures that Robinson had to endure. Some people in our league resented this action and tossed a few intemperate barbs at me, but I felt those were better answered by both players themselves.[8]

There is no question that Brown did treat his players equally (some would say equally poorly). Some have argued that Brown never fully sought racial integration, and that the various points he raised as to matters of timing and the avoiding of excessive press coverage were *post facto* rationale. The *Cleveland Press* had pointed out how weak and inexperienced the Browns were at the defensive line positions; hence recruiting Willis was purely a matter of necessity. Marion Motley also claimed that after he had been discharged from the Navy he had contacted Brown, seeking a try out with his coach's new team. Motley said Brown first turned him down, writing that he already had enough backs.[9]

Motley actually considered returning to Nevada. But Brown's backfield fortunes changed. One of the team's best running backs, Gene Fekete, had been injured in practice. Another back, Ted Fritsch, formerly of the Green Bay Packers, was a Wisconsin native and wanted to be released and return to his home. Brown acceded to Fritsch's request, and the day Fritsch left for Wisconsin, Motley arrived in the Cleveland training camp.[10]

Paul Brown's recollections make it appear as though he had a plan to achieve racial integration, but the timing may have been more accidental than anything else. Without question, though, Paul Brown was right about the greater level of journalistic inspection and pressure that someone like Jackie Robinson was going to endure. Several other factors aided Brown in his desire to minimize the extra-football dimensions of his changes. While baseball was not only far ahead of professional football in regard to public visibility in 1946, Brown's All-American Football Conference was of minimal concern even to much of the football public that summer. The league was brand new, and no one yet knew whether it would have any significance. In the 1920s, other leagues had tried to compete with the NFL, and they all failed, and there was no guarantee that the AAFC would fare any differently. The AAFC would prove significant only later, with Cleveland being the leading team, as it turned out. The league would fail, but the Browns would last. Still, in the summer before the conference had yet to play a game, no one knew what to expect. The Cleveland team had their local papers covering them, but Paul Brown's moves made little impact anywhere else in the world of sports journalism. In the summer of 1946 the NFL was dominant among reporters covering professional football.

Another factor shielding the significance of Brown's moves that summer was the fact that the senior professional football league, the NFL, had already made a similar move. When the Cleveland Rams moved to Los Angeles it created quite a stir. The Rams were the league champions in 1945. Their quarterback, Bob Waterfield, was one of the game's major stars. The West Coast press and some of Hollywood's major players began hyping the Rams. Bob Waterfield began dating the glamorous actress Jane Russell. He later married her. The Rams were grabbing headlines, and this was all to the good as far as the team's management was concerned, for amidst the publicity, ticket sales would only rise. The team was to play their home games in the Los Angeles Coliseum, a stadium which had been built for the 1932 Olympic Summer Games and which had since then been greatly under-utilized.

Several African American leaders in the Los Angeles area witnessed all the publicity about the Rams, and they intervened in a very cagy way. They pointed out that the Coliseum had been built and was being maintained with public funds, and, under the 1896 Supreme Court doctrine of "separate but equal," there was certainly no similarly sized second public arena in the city. Knowing that the city of Los Angeles was certainly not going to construct a second stadium, they made the case that a segregated sports team, playing in an arena supported by public funds, marked a legal problem.

Various NFL owners may not have been happy about it (Redskins owner George Preston Marshall certainly was not), but Rams owner Dan Reeves signed Kenneth Washington. In regard to the NFL team owners opposition, Washington himself recalled: "Reeves had the league over a barrel. The Coliseum people warned the Rams that if they practiced discrimination they couldn't use the stadium. When those NFL people began thinking about all those seats and the money they could make filling them up, they decided my kind wasn't so bad after all."[11]

The African American press was euphoric over Washington's signing. Noting how he had been tragically denied so many opportunities in the past, the *Pittsburgh Courier* noted, "Washington finally gets a break."[12] In an obvious sense that was true, but in a certain respect it was another bit of sadness. While Washington may have been one of, if not *the* greatest college football player of the 1930s, by 1946 he was 28 years old and had two bad knees, each of which had been operated on once. He wore a brace on his left knee both in practice and in games. During the 1946 season, each of Washington's knees had to be drained regularly. Dick Hyland of the *Los Angeles Times* lamented that Washington was

> a beaten-up ballplayer who is neither so strong nor so quick in his reactions as he was before the war. He has a trick leg which kept him out of games on many occasions last season [with the Hollywood Bears in 1945], and he has lost just enough of his speed to enable tackles who would have missed him or run into his murderous straight arm when he was at his best, to nail him with punishing tackles.[13]

In practice Washington showed flashes of brilliance, as well as signs of physical weakness. The Rams were the defending NFL champions, and, on paper, they had quite a backfield with Washington, Bob Waterfield, and former University of Michigan great Tom Harmon, the 1940 Heisman Trophy winner. But Washington was a particular question mark. (Tom Harmon also proved to be less the standout in the professional ranks than he had been in college, with his intervening years in the fighting of World War II taking some of his best athletic years away from him.) In the team's first game against the College All Stars, Rams coach Adam Walsh did not use Washington until the fourth quarter. Then Washington scrambled for a 10 yard gain on his first play and brought a roar from the crowd. Subsequently, though, he threw an interception and was tackled for a safety. The All Stars actually beat the champion Rams 16 to 0.

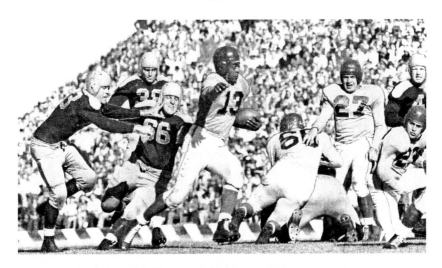

Kenneth Washington. A star runner, passer, and receiver with UCLA in the late 1930s, Kenny Washington received no offers from the NFL and played obscurely in minor league football until 1946. That year the newly relocated Los Angeles Rams signed Washington. He was thus the man who first surmounted the "color bar" in the NFL. Having incurred several knee injuries after his UCLA days, Washington was not the running back he had been. His career in the NFL would, alas, prove undistinguished.

Waterfield won the Rams starting quarterback slot. Washington's performances in exhibition games were somewhat mediocre. Walsh felt Washington was also too fragile to be used fully as a running back. He seemed to be headed for a season on the bench. In the first game of the regular season against Philadelphia, Waterfield was injured. Washington filled in and threw for a 20 yard gain. Waterfield, however, decided he could reenter the game. The pass would be Washington's only completion the entire season. Waterfield would play out the season at quarterback and win the league's MVP award. Washington put in some time at fullback. In a game against the Chicago Cardinals he ran well but hurt his knee again. The *L.A. Times* lamented that Washington's knee "will only hold together for so long.... One hard tackle at a certain spot ... and the former Bruin is generally through for the day." Washington recognized this and never whined or made excuses. "It's pretty tough in this league," he admitted. "When these linemen hit you they aren't fooling around. They play for keeps."[14]

For the entire 1946 season, Washington gained but 114 yards, caught six passes, and scored one touchdown. The next year his knees were healthier, though still tender. He ran the ball only 60 times all season. Still, he amassed 444 yards, giving him an average per carry of 7.4 yards, a league-leading figure. Merely sporadic brilliance was not going to win the affection of too many coaches, however. Washington was simply too tender physically. He played one more season, running for 301 yards and putting in some time as a defensive back.

For Washington, 1946–48 proved a most sadly mediocre career, considering both what he had been at UCLA and what barriers he was instrumental in overcoming. Cruelly, the fates had even more in store for Washington, as well, for he only lived until 1971, dying of arterial, heart, and pulmonary problems. He was only 52 years old.

For Woodrow Strode, another former UCLA star, the opening of the NFL door would prove even more inconsequential. He played one season, catching four passes. "Pro football is much tougher than college football," he admitted. "The big difference is this: in pro football you must be right all the time. You can't afford to make one mistake. If you make a mistake, you always pay for it."[15] It was a rugged life in the pros. As with respect to Washington, perhaps a younger Woodrow Strode could have made more or a mark, but Strode's best athletic days were behind him. Subsequently, he played two seasons in the Canadian Football League and then became a Hollywood actor. (In the classic gladiator movie *Spartacus*, Strode played opposite Kirk Douglas in the early part of the film. In a fight sequence, the character that Strode played had an opportunity to kill Douglas/ Spartacus but chose instead to try to kill his real enemy—Roman General Crasis, played by Lawrence Olivier. Strode's character died in the attempted assassination. In film, as in the NFL, Strode sacrificed for a cause greater than himself. His place [and pay] in the film was thus short, just like his tenure in pro football.)

In the NFL, both Washington and Strode endured a myriad of cheap shots in games and in practice, all thrust at them with a sense of entitlement, given the violent nature of the game they were playing. The verbal abuse was even worse. Was it worth it? Certainly the opening of the doors for other African American athletes marked a momentous change, but the sacrifices of men like Washington and Strode came with a heavy physical and emotional price. It is thus more than understandable when Woody Strode once ruefully commented, as he reflected on what he helped bring about in football: "If I have to integrate heaven, I don't want to go."[16]

While Washington and Strode were relatively insignificant as professional football players, their contributions to the game were enormous as they "walked point" in the assault on the entrenched segregation that had controlled the NFL for so long. There remains a con-

Woodrow Strode. The same year the Rams signed Kenny Washington, they also signed another UCLA standout—Woodie Strode. Strode played but one season in the NFL. He would go on to a successful career in Hollywood. After helping integrate the NFL, Strode once mused: "If I have to integrate heaven, I don't want to go."

tinuing argument that, for their contributions, the two deserve to be in the NFL Hall of Fame.

While Washington and Strode played to footnote status in the annals of pro football, Bill Willis and Marion Motley became real stars. They endured the same verbal assaults and physical cheap shots. In the first game of the 1946 season, when the Browns went to Florida to play the Miami Seahawks (a team for one season in the AAFC),

Willis and Motley would not make the trip, as Florida law forbade racial mixing in sports.

Motley and Willis played in all the rest of the Browns' games for the next four years, and with them helping lead the way, the Browns won the championship of the AAFC in 1946 and in each of the league's next three years of existence. In 1950, when the league folded and the Browns (along with the San Francisco 49ers and the Baltimore Colts) came over to the NFL, Cleveland was again the champion of professional football. Through the early 1950s they were the most powerful team in the game. They went to the league championship game in 1951, '52, and '53, and they won the league championship in 1954 and '55. Motley and Willis played on all the great Cleveland teams from 1946 to 1953.

While the door opened to African American players, the NFL hardly presented anything resembling an open invitation. Many teams remained all white. African Americans who gained tryouts for teams endured enormous physical and verbal abuse. Teams who brought African Americans onto their squads did so in very small increments. The means of the day were "quotas." Basketball star Bill Russell once commented about this issue. He was referring to the National Basketball Association, of course, but his sarcasm was appropriate with regard to many institutions in that era where such customs were in force. Asked whether there were quotas, he responded: "You could use two blacks if you were at home, three if you were on the road, and five if you were behind."

Just as the post–1933 segregation was a product of an unwritten gentlemen's agreement, the NFL owners appeared to enforce a limit on the number of spots that could be open to African Americans, and they continued to tolerate those owners within their little fraternity who wished to keep their own teams all-white. George Preston Marshall was the most famous "foot-dragger" here, but the other owners did not protest. This was a pattern unique neither to football nor even to the sports world in general. As doors began to open to African Americans—in schools, in businesses, in government, and in sports—quotas could be a very harsh ceiling.

To the extent that the barriers for African Americans were falling in professional football, several players made the most of the opportunity, and several teams made great strides. In the NFL progress was rather slow. Besides the Rams, the Detroit Lions were the only team to have more than one African American player before 1950. (The New York Giants, however, did sign future Hall of Famer Emlen Tunnell in 1948.) Meanwhile, the AAFC signed 13 African American players in its four years of existence. (Ironically, this was the same number that had played in the NFL from 1920 to 1933.) The Miami Seahawks had folded after one season. The team was replaced by the Baltimore Colts, and the city of Baltimore harbored many Southern prejudices. It did not have any such laws as did Miami in regard to racial competition in sports, but the Colts would actually be the only AAFC team without any black players. The Los Angeles Dons (named for one of their owners, actor Don Ameche) were under the same pressure in regard to the use of the city's Coliseum as were the Rams. They offered tryouts, and subsequently contracts, to three African American players—Ezzert Anderson, John Brown, and Bert Piggott. Cleveland added Horace Gillom to their roster in 1947. By 1947, all AAFC teams besides Baltimore and San Francisco had integrated, and the 49ers integrated the following season. Two of the most outstanding players hired at this time were Claude "Buddy" Young, who played for the New York Yankees, and Joe Perry, who starred for the San Francisco 49ers. Both were superb running backs. Young, 5'4" and one of the fastest men in the league (and in the world), continued to be the exciting runner he had been at the University of Illinois. Young's diminutive size was such that, in addition to his race, it invited "testing" by opposing linemen. But Young was never intimidated, and he played until 1955. Joe "the Jet" Perry starred for even longer. He played for 16 full seasons, amassed nearly 10,000 yards and averaged a full 5.0 yards per carry (Jim Brown's average was only slightly better—5.2).

Life was rugged for the black players who first integrated various professional football teams. The taunts and cheap shots were incessant. Joe Perry had racial slurs tossed at him relentlessly. In 1950, in a game against the Bears, Perry ran decoy in a misdirection play. With the ball on the other side of the field, and after the whistle had blown, Perry was blind-sided by Bears tackle George Conner. Perry was flattened, and he suffered two broken ribs. In 1952 Perry would flatten Conner, and from that point on the two were actually good friends! One sportswriter, Robert Smith, referred to such a resolution as a "strange result, ... one from which wiser men than I might draw a lesson on human behavior." The two were able to learn in an affirming way that the sense of the essential brutishness of the game was a fact that each realized the other fully understood, even to the point of the message being conveyed and received without words. Racial differences were thus undercut with a sense of common ground about a game each loved.[17]

At Cleveland, Marion Motley endured all the same slurs and

Bill Willis. A star lineman under Coach Paul Brown at Ohio State, Willis signed with Cleveland when Paul Brown became their first coach. Coach Brown always liked smart, lean, quick linemen, and Willis was one of the very best he ever had.

attacks. He recalled that after being called names like "alligator bait," "the only thing ... was to stop and get right up in their face and say, 'Your mother....'" How effective was this? "I'm telling you," nodded Motley, "It stopped it; 'stopped a lot of it."[18] Most of the abuse, physical as well as verbal, just had to be endured, however. Willis recalled that he made a point of winning the respect of his teammates:

> I always attempted to show respect and conducted myself in such a
> way as to demand respect from my fellow players—I never told eth-
> nic jokes, never called a teammate by a nickname unless I was cer-
> tain that I was in bounds, never rubbed a teammates hair for good
> luck, as some players did.[19]

Once he had secured that respect, and with Paul Brown coaching and
conveying that a player's race was simply not an issue on his team,
Willis learned that he could rely on teammates. In one game against
Brooklyn, Willis intervened when some of the Dodgers were piling on
Motley. When he grabbed one Brooklyn player, a fight nearly erupted.
"Keep your black hands off me!" yelled the Brooklyn player. Willis
did not release him, but then other Browns players intervened. One
teammate, Lou Rymkus, counseled Willis not to risk fighting: "If anyone gives you a bad time, you just tell us. We'll take care of him."[20]
Such team dynamics overcame prejudice (and they helped win football games), but not all coaches inspired it.

Generally, levels of violence had to be accepted as part of the
game. Players like Motley and Willis knew not only that any form of
retaliation would only invite more, they were also acutely aware of
the fact that they were helping open doors for others. Just as Branch
Rickey had warned Jackie Robinson about the onslaught of attacks
he would have to endure, Motley recalled Paul Brown telling Willis
and him: "'Now you know that you're going to be in many scrapes.
People are going to be calling you names. They're going to be nasty.
But you're going to have to stick it out....' If Willis and I had been ...
hotheads," Motley acknowledged, "it would have been another ten
years till black men got accepted in pro ball. We'd have set 'em back
ten years."[21]

As with most white players, some of the early black players in
professional football had brief, run-of-the-mill careers. Given that
many, white and black, had served in the armed forces in World War
II, some came into the professional ranks relatively late in their athletic lives. This also curtailed the longevity of many NFL careers in
the late 1940s. Some, like Bernie Jefferson, Kenny Washington, and
Woodrow Strode, only got an opportunity to play after the primes of
their athletic lives had passed. But a few, like Willis, Young, Tunnell,
Perry, and Motley, became stars, and their visibility made it ever more
ludicrous for NFL owners and coaches to ignore the wellspring of talent among African Americans.

The AAFC went bankrupt after the 1949 season. The league
folded, but three teams, the Cleveland Browns, the San Francisco
49ers, and the Baltimore Colts were absorbed into the NFL. Some

doubted the new teams were of NFL quality, but the Browns quickly laid such doubts to rest. In the first game of the 1950 season, with Willis and Motley starring, Cleveland defeated the defending NFL champion Philadelphia Eagles, and that December they won the NFL championship. The overpowering nature of the Browns and such players as Motley and Willis provided yet further evidence that they could not be cavalierly ignored or dismissed. The quality of play of many others in the AAFC was also something many NFL coaches could not overlook. With such infusion of talent around them, many NFL owners began to open further to the idea of integration. Buddy Young, Emlen Tunnell, Joe Perry, Willis, and Motley all continued their outstanding play in the NFL. Coaches could not help but notice this and realize the essential folly of believing that talent was somehow determined by skin color. Washington owner George Preston Marshall continued to cling to his backward ways, however. He stated to Sammy Baugh, "we're going to start playing black players when the Harlem Globetrotters start playing white players."[22] Thus trying to rationalize his ways, Marshall only revealed his racism to be a point of mere reaction and not action. By refusing to integrate the Redskins, while the rest of the league gradually integrated, the Redskins simply fell further and further from the perennial power they had been in the '30s and '40s and became one of the worst teams in the league in the '50s and early '60s.

It was starting in the 1950s that another hurdle began to be surmounted for African American football players. Such early stars as Buddy Young, Bill Willis, and Emlen Tunnell had played with great visibility in major colleges—Young at Illinois, Tunnell at Iowa, and Willis at Ohio State. Motley had gained a national reputation at Great Lakes. Earlier African American stars like Paul Robeson and Fritz Pollard had also been standouts in major collegiate programs too. The nation's historically black colleges and universities had yet to receive much interest or attention from NFL scouts. Part of the problem was simple ignorance—in 1950, few white coaches and scouts knew much about the football programs at schools like Grambling, Wilberforce, and Morgan State. Newspapers gave little coverage to their games. Many merely listed scores. Some did not even do that, and the African American papers that gave coverage to African American college games did not cross the desks of many NFL coaches and scouts. Beneath this ignorance, of course, lay a racist base that could not take with full seriousness the notion that the athleticism and quality of play at these schools could possibly be at the same level as at a Notre Dame or a Michigan. What was necessary was for some players to come forth whose excellence was so undeniable that everyone would have to take note. Joe Perry had gone to a small junior college in Compton, California. That changed no minds, as everyone knew there were occasional "diamonds in the rough" at the nation's many small, predominantly white schools. Historically black institutions were another matter. They were an example of what Langston Hughes more generally described as the "invisibility" of African Americans to the mainstream culture. In professional football, two men began the change in the visibility of historically black colleges. One was Tank Younger; the other was Roosevelt Brown.

Tank Younger was a graduate of Grambling University in Louisiana. He was drafted by the Rams in 1949. Then in his early years as Grambling's coach, Eddie Robinson told Younger when he was drafted: "There is one thing you have to do. You have to make it; otherwise it will be years."[23] Coach Robinson did not mean it would be years for African Americans. The focus had shifted, particularly on the Rams, as they had already integrated. Robinson meant that if Younger failed it would be years before NFL scouts and coaches again took seriously the talent that lay among the black colleges. Younger would make it, and then some. The Rams of the early 1950s were one of the league's best teams. They won their conference championship from 1949 to 1952, and in 1955. In 1951 they were league champions. Throughout these years, Younger was a main part of the Rams' running game and played effectively as well at linebacker. There were still plenty of racial incidents, however. In 1950 Los Angeles signed another African American running back, "Deacon" Dan Towler, out of Washington and Jefferson College. Towler also starred on the team. (Two black running backs in the same backfield was quite a rarity in the NFL in the early 1950s.) Towler got into a scuffle with a tackle of the Baltimore Colts named Arthur Donovan. The two held grudges against one another, and Donovan would rough up Towler whenever possible. In one game, as Donovan himself recalled, he tackled his nemesis and was hitting him with a few "extra curriculars," when suddenly he heard the downed runner yelling at him: "Hey, I ain't the Deacon." It was Younger, thus a victim of "they all look alike." Donovan turned to his teammate helping him in the extra shots and shrugged, "Hey, we got the wrong guy."[24] The racism was certainly still there, but as a result of the success of Tank Younger, no one in the NFL could ever again legitimately scoff at the notion of looking at a prospect from a little school like Grambling. Since then, of course, Grambling's contributions to the NFL have been enormous.

Roosevelt Brown had attended Morgan State in Baltimore. Morgan State had a certain presence in Baltimore because the Maryland city had no major college football team within its borders. The city's only major university—Johns Hopkins—was always at the top in lacrosse, but it enjoyed vastly lesser status in all other sports, including football. The University of Maryland lay 40 miles to the south of Baltimore and was always a bit more the team of the Washington, D.C. area than of Baltimore. More than any other school, the Naval Academy was actually the team that historically occupied Baltimore's college football fans and sports media. But Annapolis was also 30 miles away, leaving the Academy less central to the football culture of Baltimore than was, for example, USC in Los Angeles or Ohio State in Columbus. Morgan State was thus the biggest and best college football program in the city. Certainly not every white fan then rooted for Morgan State, but the city's two white newspapers and the *Baltimore Afro-American* covered them, and a considerable number of white fans followed them (as, of course, did virtually all African American football fans in the area). The school had a wider visibility and appeal in Baltimore than did Grambling in New Orleans, Lincoln in Philadelphia, Tuskeegee in Birmingham and Montgomery, or Morehouse in Atlanta. Morgan State also enjoyed particular success in the post-war years, and this heightened its visibility. With this successful program in the city of Baltimore, rather than tucked away in some little Southern backwater, the Eastern press then came to have at least some awareness of the quality football played there.

In the early 1950s Roosevelt Brown was an outstanding lineman at Morgan, on both offense and defense. In 1953 the New York Giants gave him a tryout after drafting him—in the 27th round. The fact that it was New York where Brown broke in would further erode the barriers of neglect and ignorance that had plagued black college programs. Los Angeles and others had already integrated, but it would be many more years before Los Angeles would rival the East as a national media and cultural center. In 1953 New York was unquestionably the media center of the nation in regard to all areas of sports and entertainment. If Roosevelt Brown could make an impact with the Giants, there would be much visibility, and much could change in the NFL.

Upon his arrival at the Giants camp, Brown turned heads. His strength and fundamental skills were unsurpassed. At 6'3", 250 pounds, and with a 29" waist, Brown certainly impressed many of his comparatively fat competitors at camp. What truly amazed everyone on the Giants was Brown's speed. Since 1946, Paul Brown's methods had been increasingly dominant in professional football, and he had always emphasized the value of speed. Roosevelt Brown was some-one the Giants could use to begin to compete with their conference rival in Cleveland. Frank Gifford was the fastest back on the Giants, and he quickly learned, and freely acknowledged, that Roosevelt Brown, an offensive tackle no less, was as fast as he was. Brown's speed, strength, and techniques were second to none. He could play both offense and defense, and sometimes did, playing some defensive middle guard as well as offensive tackle. He was a true standout on the offensive line, making all-pro at offensive tackle year after year. Brown became a star both in pro football and in the nation's media center. He was one of the major reasons the Giants became a pro football power by the mid and late 1950s, displacing the Cleveland Browns as the best team in the Eastern Conference. Along with Tank Younger, Brown's undeniable stature also underscored the growing under-standing of the quality of play at schools like Morgan State and Grambling. Brown's speed and size particularly made NFL coaches note the previously unseen possibility of big men being so fast. They had seldom seen such athleticism in the major college ranks.

With the presence of stars like Roosevelt Brown and Tank Younger, black colleges began to make inroads into the NFL. It would still take many years for them to gain a fulsome position in the outlooks of NFL scouting systems. A major stumbling block here was that NFL team managers were slow to employ African Americans as scouts, even though by the late 1950s there were sufficient numbers of retired African American players who could do the job. Player rosters were tough enough to crack; coaching, scouting, and front office staffs were yet another barrier.

With Paul Brown's continuing influence in helping form much of the character of the modern professional game, the emphasis on the significance of speed grew as other coaches had to take note of his methods and preferences. With speed and not race as a concern, coaches looked wherever they could to find it. Here a great many African American players began to find openings. Ollie Matson had been a 1952 Olympic bronze medalist in the 400 meters and a gold medalist in the 1600-meter relay. He played for several seasons with the Chicago Cardinals, who unfortunately provided him with little team support to showcase his talents as a runner, receiver, punt and kick returner, and defensive back. The Los Angeles Rams wanted Matson badly, and in 1958 they actually gave up eight players and a draft choice in exchange for him. The trade market had never before revealed any player, white or black, to be regarded so valuably.

As talent, irrespective of race, came ever more to the fore, other stars entered the league and made major impacts, athletically and otherwise. In 1956 the Baltimore Colts found Lenny Moore, a can't-miss star out of Penn State and a Baltimore native, whose success brought Baltimore fans, white and black, together in adoration of such a great talent. The next season the Colts also signed Jim Parker out of Ohio State. Like Lenny Moore, Parker's college credentials were unassailable. Ohio State's Woody Hays always said Parker was the best offensive lineman he had ever coached. Parker became one of the (some would say *the*) greatest offensive interior linemen in the history of game. Parker made all-pro eight times, and he did so at two positions, as in mid-career he switched from offensive tackle to guard and continued to make all-pro. He became the first interior offensive lineman to make the Pro Football Hall of Fame. Parker's contributions to the Colts were enormous. When the Colts began in the NFL in 1953 they were a poor team. By 1956 they had climbed to "good" status. It was in 1957 that they leapt into contender status. They already had John Unitas, Raymond Berry, Alan Ameche, and Gino Marchetti. Rookie Jim Parker's anchoring of the offensive line was the new major factor here. In addition to Parker's success as a player, he became one of the Colts' team leaders on the field and in the locker room. He was then one of the first African American players not only to make NFL teams and not only to star, but to become, by virtue of personality and character, a leader among all his teammates, one to whom others looked with friendship and admiration.

Barely a decade elapsed between Kenny Washington's signing with the Rams and Jim Parker's emergence as a leader on the Baltimore Colts. African American athletes had surmounted many, many obstacles, and many endured much to do it. There was much more to be overcome, but aside from the fancies in the minds of a few old codgers like Washington's George Preston Marshall, there was certainly no turning back.

Eleven

The Life and Death of Big Daddy and the Decline of Marion Motley

By the mid 1950s, many African Americans began coming into the National Football League, and gained respect and admiration via the finest athletic as well as intellectual and personal credentials. Jim Brown was the greatest such figure here, but there were many others. The presence of such compelling figures made earlier resistance to integration look ever more silly. While some novels and movie scripts may characterize social change in such a straightforward manner, there would be complicating elements and personalities (as would be found in a cross section of players of *any* race or background) that would invariably emerge from the ranks of African Americans as their numbers swelled in the NFL.

Back in the 1930s, writers like Richard Wright raised such issues in his novel *Native Son*. At the point when football and other sports and institutions were integrating, James Baldwin extended such a theme in *Blues for Mr. Charlie*. As in sports, the world of jazz had similarly compelled a public to contend with the brilliance of various stars. With figures like Billie Holiday and Charlie Parker, the recognition of their artistic brilliance had to occur in cognizance of the violent self-destructiveness that surrounded each of them. Many, however, simply preferred to ignore the questions such troubled lives raise. Worse, some preferred to Romanticize such self-destructiveness or even cast it as inherent in the habits of an entire race. The violent world of football presented some unsettling examples too, examples which bring forth issues which have never been eclipsed and continue to present vexing questions to all thoughtful people.[1]

Having integrated with Kenny Washington, Woody Strode, Tank

Younger, and Dan Towler, the NFL's Los Angeles Rams continued to innovate and break down barriers of race. In the scouting of talent, a major "find" came in 1953 in the massive person of Eugene "Big Daddy" Lipscomb. Lipscomb was not only not a product of one of the nation's major predominantly white college programs, he had not "merely" attended a little-known black college either.[2] Lipscomb was a product of no college; he never even graduated from high school. He had served in the United States Marine Corps, and while stationed at Camp Pendleton in California, the base's track coach took notice of him. Lipscomb was apparently seen picking up a 40 pound piece of cannon equipment with his finger tips like it was a feather. Snapped up by the track coach, Lipscomb became his Marine Division's shot put champion. He was also recruited to play defensive end on the base's football team. He was 6'6", weighed 270 pounds and was as fast as any player on the squad. He was remarkable indeed.

The notices which Lipscomb received while playing on the West Coast at Camp Pendleton crossed the desk of the public relations director, subsequently the general manager, of the Los Angeles Rams—Pete Rozelle. Rozelle signed Lipscomb for the 1953 season. Lipscomb was indeed phenomenally strong and quick, and his "wing span" when his arms were outstretched measured seven feet. As a defensive lineman, his rush and pursuit of offensive backs was unlike anything football had seen.

Lipscomb's combination of speed and size eclipsed even that of such stars as Roosevelt Brown. Coming as he did out of such obscurity, Lipscomb's awesome talents seemed all the more freakish. One oddity: Lipscomb could easily carry other players on his shoulders and still run effectively. This was no mere joke to amuse teammates at the end of a hard day's practice. Lipscomb and a teammate could use the stunt effectively to try to block field goals. They actually did it once against the Bears, much to the anger and chagrin of Coach George Halas. On the play, Lipscomb even ran after the blocked kick with his teammate still on his shoulders. He was, however, quickly tripped. With Halas's stern urging, the league quickly outlawed Lipscomb's tactic.

A problem for Lipscomb in his early years in the NFL was that he lacked some technical lineman skills and was thus susceptible to draws, traps, and misdirections. Opposing linemen learned that while it was fruitless to take Lipscomb on in a match of strength, they could get under his massive shoulders and arms and let his own momentum carry him off to one side or another. Opponents also learned they could not only get under Big Daddy's shoulders, they could get under

Gene "Big Daddy" Lipscomb. Big Daddy was one of the first linemen in football who was both big and fast. Standing 6'7" and weighing 295 lbs., he was also faster than most running backs in the league. Truly frightening to opponents (as well as to many teammates), Big Daddy died of a heroin overdose at the age of 31.

his skin, not so much with racial taunts, although there were still plenty of those, but with references like "dummy." It was a risk, though, as "Big Daddy" was hardly anyone with whom any opponent ever wanted to get in a fight, and he had a definite and frightening mean streak, to say the least.

While showing incredible physical talent and potential, Lipscomb also quickly developed a notorious reputation for off-field behavior. This included well-deserved reputations as a womanizer and a drinker. As a result, early in the 1956 season the Rams concluded Lipscomb was uncontrollable, and they released him. He was eagerly snapped up by the Baltimore Colts, whose coach Weeb Eubank always had a keen eye for talent and believed personal behavior issues to be secondary. At Baltimore, Lipscomb learned solid defensive line techniques, largely from teammates Art Donovan and Gino Marchetti. There he blossomed into an all-pro player, and the Colts' defensive line of Donovan, Marchetti, Lipscomb, and Don Joyce was arguably the best of their time, and one of the best of all time. In Baltimore, Lipscomb's unbelievable talent and football feats became legend. While linebackers usually lead a team in tackles, Lipscomb was always the Colts' leader here. In the 1959 championship game against the Giants, Lipscomb was pursuing quarterback Charlie Connerly. Lipscomb leaped in the air to block a pass, and Connerly reacted by dumping a little flair pass to Frank Gifford. Lipscomb landed, turned, and ran Gifford down from behind before he had reached the line of scrimmage. On another occasion against Green Bay, from his defensive tackle position, Lipscomb chased a speedy running back named Tom Moore 40 yards into the end zone and knocked down a potential touchdown pass. Coach Weeb Eubank and defense coach Charlie Winner wanted to make Lipscomb a linebacker, but he was simply too valuable on the defensive line. The greatest running back, Jim Brown, confessed that Big Daddy was the only football player who ever made him feel genuine fear. Big Daddy scared a lot of people—and not just on the field.

While the legends surrounding "Big Daddy's" playing were astounding, his off-field activities were even more fabled. He was a man with an insatiable appetite for liquor, for women, and for high living. Previously there had certainly been plenty of such living-on-the-edge characters in football, as well as in all sports, but the specter of such extreme impropriety in a black man from the "other side of the tracks" touched raw nerves, particularly given the way that Lipscomb's saga turned out.

Big Daddy was the first modern football player to present some of the elements of pathology that come with many with troubled pasts. Race, per se, was not the root here, though many wanted (and still want) to see it so. The real issue was poverty. Race was an ancillary part of the picture, of course, because, as a result of racism, African Americans are generally poorer, and, to say the least, the slurs of racism salt many of the wounds of poverty. With greater levels of poverty, the pathologies that can accompany it invariably arise in a cross section of poor people, black and white, in sports and everywhere else. Like a Richard Wright character, with tinges of a Joe Lillard or, even more, of a Jack Johnson, Gene Lipscomb had a fearsome nature that extended from a troubled background which had created a complicated and quixotic personality.

Gene Lipscomb never knew his father. He grew up with only his mother, and when he was eleven years old she was stabbed to death (47 times) by her boyfriend while waiting for a bus on the streets of Detroit. A stern maternal grandfather took him in, and he compelled the boy to hold jobs in order to pay rent for room and board. One year, while in high school, Lipscomb worked the midnight to 7:00 A.M. shift in a steel mill every night before going to school. Always insecure about his size (in the sixth grade he was 6'4") and about being regarded as a dummy, Lipscomb developed traits of both extreme kindness and uncontrollable rage. Sports gave him an outlet, and he may have caught the eye of some college football coaches, but the fates were already conspiring against Lipscomb. Because he had played some basketball and softball for pay in summers, Lipscomb lost his football eligibility as he approached his senior year in high school. This was when, on the advice of a high school coach, he joined the Marines, which led him directly to professional football. Although the Marines gave Lipscomb some grounding, within him were the unresolved elements of sadness, insecurity, kindness, and rage. With the money and adoration that came with pro football, particularly with the stardom he achieved in Baltimore, the lures of fast times, fast women, and liquor would be irresistible.

While Lipscomb was terrorizing the National Football League, he was even more a maniac in the night life of Baltimore. When the Colts, rather stupidly many said, traded Lipscomb to Pittsburgh in 1961 he continued his magnificent play as well as his outrageous drinking and womanizing. He was married three times and was never faithful. It was said he took on women by the half dozen. Children loved him, and he was always kind, gentle, and generous with them, as he was to many poor people on the streets. Meanwhile, he caroused like no one else. The Steelers' hard drinking quarterback Bobby Layne used to buy drinks for all who went out with him, except for Lipscomb. Instead of buying Big Daddy a drink, Layne would buy him a whole bottle.

Even after being traded to Pittsburgh, Lipscomb continued to live in Baltimore. Children all over the city absolutely adored him. Many a skid row bum had warm coats and occasional bedrooms in which to sleep as a result of Big Daddy (sometimes it was Big Daddy's bedroom, while Big Daddy himself slept on the couch). Lipscomb was an enormous presence and made a difference in the lives of many on the run-down streets of downtown Baltimore, and it was in this ghetto that he died on May 10, 1963, at the age of 31.

The details of Big Daddy's death still remain somewhat mysterious. The actual cause of his death was a heroin overdose, but from there lies nothing but controversy. The morning that Lipscomb died, radio news programs in Baltimore broadcast that doctors found many needle marks on Lipscomb's arms. This naturally led many to conclude that he had been using drugs. Then various people who knew him began to tell stories of how this did not ring true for them, as Big Daddy had always been afraid of needles. Some speculated that a man with whom Lipscomb had been partying that night, Timothy Black may have administered heroin to him in order to rob him. Seven hundred dollars was supposedly stolen from Lipscomb the night he died.

Timothy Black, himself a heroin addict, stated that Lipscomb had been using heroin three times a week for about six months prior to his death. Lipscomb's widow, Cecelia, and several former teammates, including Lenny Moore, denied that Lipscomb used heroin or any drugs. They emphasized the point that Lipscomb was always afraid of needles and that Black's story had shifted at various times. Black's story did indeed shift. Black first said he left Lipscomb after partying with him on the night of May 10, went to an all-night diner, then came back and found him overdosed and comatose. Later he said that he had "cooked" the heroin, watched Lipscomb inject some into himself and then begin to react strangely. Black said he shot up the rest of the heroin himself but also tried to revive Lipscomb with ice and with saline injections, finally calling an ambulance. Whatever the circumstances, Lipscomb never came out of the coma into which he had slipped.

Various Baltimore friends and reporters have been in virtual unison in their discounting of Black's story. Of course, they were not present when the tragedy occurred. Such unity can invite speculation that people have tried consciously to forge a story kind to Lipscomb's memory. To this end, many have pointed out the shifting nature of Black's version, and added that, as the Baltimore police had used Black as an informant, the police may have preferred to protect him and maintain the line that Lipscomb was a drug user and not a victim of Black's thievery. This idea is not unbelievable, but however politically unpopular, it is somewhat doubtful that the police would compromise a high profile death case for the sake of such a low-scale informant as Black, with a checkered heroin-using past to boot. In any case, when people on various sides of an issue have to rely on notions that some are concocting conspiracies, it is clear that solid evidence has run out.

What has never been brought forth to the mix of stories surrounding the death of Big Daddy is the point that Lipscomb may have become a so-called "medical junkie" as a result of football. James Donnelly, a former reporter with the *Baltimore Sun*, claimed that, while on the sidelines with a press pass at Colts games, he witnessed Lipscomb coming out of games in various degrees of pain, from injuries and cheap shots, and often being given pain injections.[3] Such medical practices in the NFL were more blatant back then. This, of course, contradicts the notion that Lipscomb was afraid of needles (or at least the idea that he could not overcome the fear when in pain). The large and vocal chorus citing Lipscomb's needle fears here can make some wonder whether various people have a bit too conveniently seized upon this as a point of denial.

Certainly, if Lipscomb had been taking pain killers during his years of playing, and perhaps had begun to take more as he aged, he could have been in a position to be in need, psychologically as well as physically, of some form of pain killers in the off-season. And by the time he was 30–31 years old, the off-season aches and pains of professional football may have been wearing on him as they do so many others. The chronology of Timothy Black's claim—that Lipscomb had been using heroin for six months before he died—would place the beginning of his alleged drug use almost exactly at the point when his last season with the Pittsburgh Steelers had ended.

In contrast to those who found it inconceivable that a person of Lipscomb's character could use drugs, there is also the clear evidence that he had many sides to his character, to the point indeed of bordering on schizophrenia. When a Rams teammate, Harry Thompson, was in a car with Lipscomb, another driver cut them off. Lipscomb leaped from the car and rammed his fist through the other driver's window. Then, back with Thompson, his bleeding hand wrapped in a towel, Lipscomb confessed, "I wish I hadn't done that." Another Ram teammate, "Deacon" Dan Towler, who had tried to minister to Lipscomb, said that Big Daddy was indeed "like Dr. Jekyll and Mr. Hyde. His animal nature was unchecked."[4] From his unknown father, to his unexpressed feelings about his murdered mother, to his brutal grandfather, Lipscomb was indeed an emotional volcano. Having squelched many of his true emotions, and with these emotions then running his life (a great combination for a Marine or an NFL defensive lineman), he spent his adulthood showing only certain sides of himself to people, hiding others, and turning to rage whenever anyone approached areas he subconsciously deemed off limits. Many who thought they knew Big Daddy may have not seen some of the really ugly sides in their rawest form. There, perhaps, was where the heroin needles lay, at the point of his greatest fears and pain, which came out as the aches of an aging player in a violent game were providing him with new and frightening senses of his own fragile mortality (as well as his mother's).

Likely no one will ever know the full circumstances of Big Daddy's death, but his saga unearthed for pro football, and for other elements of a society trying to deal with the heritage of racial and class injustice, elements of the ugliest sides of life which can come forth with people of all backgrounds, but which reveal themselves especially among those who, amidst worlds of poverty, crime, and despair, grow up with severe emotional traumas and scars. Those who wanted to keep the game of football "safe," an obvious contradiction given the savagery such a violent game nurtures, could use the life of Big Daddy as an excuse to chortle about the futility of reaching out in such a manner. In contrast to the old-fashioned segregationists, the straightforward solution of making a market place of talent open to all simply opens that market place to all psychological make-ups which random chance will invariably link to those few with remarkable levels of athletic talent. The sad saga of Big Daddy was one of the most extreme forms of this mixture of beauty and ugliness, much like the stories of artists like Billie Holiday and Charlie Parker. The unresolvable dualities in such flawed geniuses continue to manifest themselves in many other areas of life. Some even romanticize these sorts of figures, as though drug addiction provides a way of getting in touch with some deeper elements regarding the meaning of life. (Billie Holiday, for one, did not agree; to her, drug addiction was simply endless pain.) The sports world remains a visible area where self-destructive anger and drug addiction remain vexing problems which compel attention and defy easy solutions. For forms of destructive anger have close links to some of the instincts that make a good athlete, especially in a violent sport. Meanwhile, drugs remain an ever-present lure in sports, as well as in society at large, and will remain so as long as there is money to be made through them.

The story of Big Daddy is one of the most extreme in regard to how a sports figure can be used, or use himself up, amidst the inner crosscurrents of a traumatized, unintegrated personality. Because the problems inherent in such complex behavior are so difficult, if not

impossible, to handle, many leaders can easily fall back onto rhetorical shrugs at the vagaries of the market place. Such rhetoric can lead
many in the sports world, after paying a little lip service to the notions
of the need for compassion for the unfortunate, to move on from there
with the simple notion that some people make bad choices. In this
spirit, the sports world has been littered with people who fell into
neglect after their athleticism faded and were no longer of any use to
coaches and managers. Marion Motley himself, despite all he contributed to the game and to his team, suffered such a fate.

Half-jokingly, Green Bay Packer players under Vince Lombardi
used to say of their coach: "He treats us all equally—like dogs." Paul
Brown showed a certain proclivity along these lines. Cleveland players usually felt themselves to be part of Brown's "system." Brown had
many purely mathematical measurements of his players' abilities. This
was part of why Brown did not care if a player was white or black.
But players' thoughts about football matters were also of little interest to Coach Brown. The resulting sense among players of being
regarded as cogs in a machine then came forth in other ways, ways
which were quite painful to Marion Motley. Motley freely acknowledged how playing under Brown was a joy in that Brown was the best
technician in the business, and he allowed no issue to be made of race.
The "non-personal" way Brown went about his work could also be
impersonal.

With Motley and Otto Graham, the Browns won championships
every year from 1946 to 1950. Then, during pre-season practice in
1951, Motley injured his knee. He had hurt his knee back in his college days at Nevada, but this had healed, and he had largely been
injury free during his first professional years in Cleveland. In the 1948
season he averaged 8.8 yards per carry. The day Motley injured his
knee it swelled significantly. The trainer told Brown that Motley should
take a couple of days of rest. Brown responded tersely: "No. No, he
can come out and run a little bit. If he can't run, he can hop around."
Motley did what he was told. Altering his stride to favor his bad knee,
Motley hurt his other knee as well. A doctor drained two pans of
water off his knees and again prescribed several days rest. Motley
recalled:

> So I went back to camp thinking I'm going to get a rest, but after I'd
> stayed off the field for one day, Paul Brown told me, "you get your
> suit on and be out here." I put on my equipment ..., and then Paul
> said, "All right, Motley, Get in here. I want you to run some." I tried
> to, but my knees locked up on me and swelled up on me big as a bal-
> loon. I had to have the water taken off again.

... after the [first pre-season] game I couldn't walk out of [the stadium]. I had to lean against a wall while they brought my car to me. I couldn't move. I always had knee trouble after that, and football became a job.[5]

Motley's knees were never the same. He played the 1951 season in pain and then suffered through two more painful years. He sat out the 1954 season, but in 1955, needing the income, he tried to come back. Paul Brown recognized that Motley's legs were no longer strong enough for him to play fullback, but he hoped Motley could still play linebacker. This did not work out either. Finally Brown traded Motley to Pittsburgh, where he played one futile year with the Steelers. The trade to Pittsburgh was unceremonious, and Brown admitted that in the trading of Motley, "I did not handle the situation well.... I didn't have the courage to tell Marion first hand that we traded him, and before I could think of a better solution, he found out from another source, deeply hurting him."[6] Motley would endure more hurt, despite his many contributions to the game.

Those who had seen Motley play in the AAFC lamented how NFL fans, as much as they admired Motley's play, never saw him at anything close to his best. "The people who are talking about the Motley who played in the NFL—on two bad knees," lamented Lou Saban, who played with Motley in Cleveland and later coached the Buffalo Bills and the Denver Broncos, "the Motley they saw was just a shadow of the old Motley, even when he made All-Pro in '50 and led the league in running. Don't forget, he was 26 years old in his rookie year—in 1946."[7]

Motley never whined about his knees, or about the fact, as many football people have attested, that his talents were underutilized in the conservative trap-and-pass offensive scheme of Paul Brown.[8] Motley's top salary, in 1953, was $11,500. He could have complained on this score too, but he never did. When his knee injuries ended his playing, Motley had little savings and had to look for other work, as did many veterans. Motley asked Paul Brown for a job coaching or scouting. Brown tersely advised him to look for a job in a local steel mill. The Browns' door remained closed to Motley as long as Paul Brown was the coach.

After the 1962 season, when Art Modell bought the team and ultimately replaced Paul Brown with Blanton Collier, Motley was hired briefly to help scout players at black colleges. But, said Motley, the work was minimal. "The Browns were just sending me [to black schools] as an appeasement, to keep me from saying anything." Modell flatly told Motley that his only use to the team would be in helping to sign players (who, if they were good, were getting competing offers from the rival American Football League). Motley never had anything to do with the Cleveland Browns after that, and when the team hired an outsider, Bob Nussbaumer, an undistinguished journeyman player in the late '40s and early '50s with the Packers, Redskins, and Cardinals, to help coach and scout, Motley made his feelings known to the press. He blasted the Browns for their ingratitude and claimed that race lay within the neglect. Modell reacted defensively, in much the same tone he would later employ when moving the Browns to Baltimore. He claimed Motley had done him "an injustice," adding, "I'm not prejudiced. I always tried to help the Negro. I give to their community fund." Motley was hardly impressed or mollified.[9]

When Motley's former teammate, quarterback Otto Graham, became head coach of the Washington Redskins in 1967, he asked Motley to assist with some coaching and scouting. Graham's tenure with Washington did not last, however. Elsewhere, Motley's finances never panned out. He owned a bar in Cleveland, but it did not succeed. In 1978 he tried to coach a team of female players in an abortive attempt to start a women's football league. Otherwise he worked for the United States Post Office and was a supervisor for the Ohio State Lottery System. In 1997 he suffered an incapacitating stroke and died in the summer of 1999. He never stopped wearing his Cleveland Browns jacket, as he always pointed out: "I earned it."[10]

African American football players of Motley's generation could crack the player market, but they could not become coaches, scouts, or managers. That would take more time. The sense of African Americans' capabilities for coaching, scouting, or front office work contrasted with the often condescending view as to their considerable "natural" athletic talents. When Los Angeles Dodgers official Al Campanis made the infamous statement in 1987 about African Americans lacking "some of the necessities" for baseball management, he was revealing what many sports team owners and managers harbored long after the color line was broken among players. Cincinnati Reds owner Marge Schott and the Washington Redskins' George Preston Marshall were the most extreme, uncloseted racists, but the sad fact was that they were not unique. They were merely less subtle than most.

While there is no proof, a fascinating pattern in the evolution of the predominant major league baseball strategies came forth in the decade after Jackie Robinson broke the color line. One of Robinson's many strengths as a player lay in his ability to terrorize the opposition once he got on base. Broadcaster Red Barber once said only Ty Cobb could intimidate an opposing team as effectively as Robinson, a comparison which, if he had heard it, would certainly have made the racist Cobb's blood boil (let's hope he heard it). At the very point that Robinson and others had broken the color line in major league baseball, managers tended toward strategies which de-emphasized the speed and finesse styles of the game. It was not until the emergence of the "Go-Go" Chicago White Sox of the late 1950s (who won the American League pennant in 1959, the only non–Yankee pennant from 1955 through 1964) that the national pastime saw a reemergence of what had been called "scientific baseball." Was Jackie Robinson's and other African Americans' new presence in the game a motive here in the decade of de-emphasis of speed and finesse?

With Paul Brown's undeniable success between 1946 and 1955, football was, unlike major league baseball, moving toward speed, but there were other tendencies in professional football that augured against the rise in numbers of African American football players. Teams in both baseball and football employed quotas. Baseball also erected racial walls with predominating strategies that shied away from the speed and finesse game for which African Americans were allegedly well-suited. Football reflexively turned to an odd mentality which defined various positions racially. It was in the 1940s and 1950s that football people began the mythologies of racially appropriate positions. Few ever bothered to consider that back in the days of seg-regation, African Americans had obviously played all the game's posi-tions at black colleges and on black professional teams (and coached and managed as well). What became an orthodoxy (and a nervously told series of tasteless jokes) involved a setting aside of certain posi-tions at which there emerged the mythology that only whites could play. Quarterback was the most visible one here, but equally segre-gated were the positions of center, middle linebacker, and defensive safety. These were the center-of-the-field spots that, as the mythology had it, required intelligence as well as athletic ability. Positions to the outside, like cornerback, wide receiver, and offensive guard and tackle, were regarded as more "instinctive" and could rely on "natural" strength and ability. The racism within these vocabularies and patterns was obvious, and not just in hindsight. Various African American play-ers, like Kenny Washington and Wilmeth Sidat Singh, had excelled at quarterback. The kind of play that African Americans symbolized in baseball was the very sort of brains-over-brawn style of which foot-ball scions were nervously asserting blacks were incapable.

There were a few cracks in these walls. In 1953 the Baltimore Colts and the Chicago Bears both used African Americans at quar-terback. In October of that season, Bears' coach George Halas inserted

Willie Thrower at quarterback. Thrower had led his Pittsburgh area high school to two Western Pennsylvania Interscholastic League titles in 1946 and 1947. From there he had been the first black quarterback in the Big Ten; he helped Michigan State to a national championship in 1952, leading the team to a key win over Notre Dame. With the Bears, Thrower played one brief stint, completing three of eight passes for twenty-seven yards and throwing one interception. Halas then put in another quarterback, George Blanda, and Thrower never played quarterback again. But he was the first African American to play the lead offensive position in the NFL since the rag-tag, single wing days of the 1920s.

Late in the 1953 season the Baltimore Colts found their two mediocre quarterbacks, Fred Enke and Jack Del Bello, injured. Amidst cheers of "Let George do it!" the team turned to all-purpose player George Taliaferro, who was otherwise a leading rusher, pass receiver, and punt and kickoff returner. Taliaferro then started at quarterback for several games and thus became the first African American in the NFL to start at quarterback. He played as well as any quarterback on the team that year. In 1955 Charles Brackins threw two passes for the Green Bay Packers. From that point, no African American played quarterback in professional football until 1968, when Marlin Briscoe played for Denver.

Middle linebacker was another position that remained notoriously all-white for many years. Kansas City's Willie Lanier expunged all notions that African Americans could not play middle linebacker, but that was not until the late 1960s.[11]

The sense of racially "appropriate" positions remained influential in professional (and major college) football for many years. Few blacks played quarterback. After Briscoe's brief stint, Joe Gilliam was the next African American starting quarterback. He played for Pittsburgh in 1974. The reaction to Joe Gilliam gaining the starting role was enormous. Gilliam received many threats and large quantities of hate mail. When the team faltered under his leadership, and Terry Bradshaw re-emerged as the team's quarterback, many football people and Steeler fans (who would all deny any racism) chortled over how Gilliam's tenure worked out. A few other African Americans played well at quarterback, notably Warren Moon and Randall Cunningham, and the barrier began to crumble, but it would not be until the 1987 season and the January 1988 Super Bowl, when Doug Williams of the Washington Redskins was the star of the game in a lopsided massacre of the Denver Broncos, that much of the mythology of blacks somehow lacking some of the necessary ingredients to be successful quarterbacks in the NFL finally subsided for good.

With regard to the racial stereotyping of players and positions, where the patterns of racism were strongest, teams suffered in the win/loss columns. Where the patterns were broken, the teams succeeded and then laughed merrily at those who clung to old, illogical ways.

Twelve

George Marshall's Last Stand

Amidst the many crosscurrents of change in the social composition of professional football between 1945 and 1962, one NFL team remained steadfastly mired in the pre–World War II ways of segregation—the Washington Redskins. The reason was simple—the owner. George Preston Marshall had been the Redskins owner since 1934. A native West Virginian with considerable Confederate sensibilities, he grew up in early 20th-century Washington, D.C., a city which then followed strict customs and patterns of racial segregation. Marshall had moved the Redskins from Boston to Washington after the 1936 season, and he did so with a conscious sense of marketing the Redskins as the NFL's team of the South. The plan worked, as the Redskins became not just the team of football fans in Washington, D.C. and its immediate suburbs, but of football fans throughout Virginia, the Carolinas and other parts of the South. For years Marshall cultivated this by playing many pre-season games in Virginia and North Carolina. The sensibilities of Southern whites were not necessary inducements for Marshall to resist any form of racial integration. No matter his fans, the owner harbored clear racist attitudes throughout his life, but the combination of redneck owner and redneck fans was mutually reinforcing, particularly as the winds of change blew everywhere else in the NFL and about the nation.

As the rest of the league integrated, Marshall conspicuously resisted. In 1962 he made his adamant declaration: "We'll start signing Negroes when the Harlem Globetrotters start signing whites."[1] Former running back Bobby Mitchell recalled, from his seasons with the Cleveland Browns in the late 1950s and early 1960s, one matter which always struck him when playing in Washington—at the Redskins' Griffith Stadium one looked around and saw "no black folks in the grandstands." Marshall not only kept his team all white, no African Americans, it seemed, took tickets, hawked souvenirs, or even sold peanuts.[2] Paul Brown always regarded Marshall as parsimonious and downright loutish. When the AAFC merged with the NFL, Brown noted how Marshall tried to shortchange the surviving AAFC teams. At League meetings, Brown said Marshall was always "obnoxious ... [He] slept through most meetings and had to be briefed when [he arrived] late. When the rest were [then] tired he would try to work deals, and he would try to peek at everyone's lists at draft meetings."[3]

Marshall's boorishness, his racism, and his resistance to integration, like the pattern of the indulgences of Klansmen among the citizenry of small Southern towns in the Jim Crow era,

George Preston Marshall. Long-time owner of the Boston and Washington Redskins, Marshall led the NFL's team owners' ban of African-American players in the 1930s. When the league began to integrate, Marshall would be the last holdout, with the Redskins suffering much demoralization as a result. Marshall would not integrate the Redskins until 1962, and then only because of some artfully applied pressure from members of the Kennedy Administration.

were things that the other NFL owners thought it would somehow be impolite to challenge. By the 1950s, Marshall was one of the senior citizens in the league's leadership, and his stature somehow commanded indulgence, no matter what the nature of his behavior. Such a pattern was an illustration of what Martin Luther King was arguing at that very time—that it was not only the racism of the white extremists that was problematic to the cause of civil rights; just as significant was the passivity of whites who believed they harbored positive attitudes about civil rights but were unwilling to step forth and do anything about the abhorrent actions and views they knew to be in their midst. Lots of communities suffer from such cancerous passivity. Such behavior is supported by economic comfort, and it is usually rationalized, nervously, along lines that those who seek to challenge the status quo are somehow showing bad manners, are trying to upset the established order, and should recognize that the changes they desire would somehow come about more easily if they did *not* agitate as they did.

History shows little logic in such views. If there was no agitation against the status quo, the same people who fuss at the alleged bad manners of the activists would dismiss any criticism of old ways as quantitatively insignificant. There will always be an anxious timidity among those who are generally apathetic when not economically affected by an immoral state of affairs. It often then takes efforts by the affected minorities, with help from the outside, to change things, all to the indignant shock of those content with passivity. This was the nature of the civil rights movement in the United States in the 1950s and '60s, and the end of segregation on the Washington Redskins was a mini-example within this.

While refusing to integrate, Marshall's Redskins had fallen precipitously in their standing in the Eastern Conference of the NFL. In the 1930s and 1940s, when the entire league was segregated, Marshall's teams were perennial powers. Having quarterback/safety/punter Sammy Baugh on his roster was a major factor here, of course. Baugh retired just as the NFL was tearing down its racial walls. Marshall's Redskins remained white and, with their owner's refusal to tap one of the well-springs of talent that the other teams were exploiting, the Redskins grew comparatively mediocre. In four seasons from 1958 through 1961 they won a total of nine games while losing 37 and tying four. Unlike other pathetic teams of the era, like baseball's 1962 New York Mets, there was no *esprit de corps* on this hapless football team because of their beloved failures. The Redskins were just plain lousy. They knew it, and they had little desire to play with any extraordinary level of spirit.

In addition to his open racism, various actions by Marshall contributed markedly to the Washington Redskins' malaise. In regard to scheduling, for example, Marshall did not favor the league placing a franchise in Baltimore in 1953, just 45 miles away from Washington. He was always worried about the popularity of the Baltimore Colts cutting into his market. Each of the two divisions of the NFL played every team in their own division twice a season. A few games with teams in the other division rounded out the schedule. The selection of these inter-divisional matches varied year to year in the league, except in one instance. Marshall used his influence with the other league owners to see to it that Washington would always play one regular season game against Baltimore. He believed such an annual game would keep the rivalry and distinction between the two markets from eroding at his end. The result, however, was that year after year the hapless Redskins of the late '50s and '60s had to play the Colts, who, with Johnny Unitas, Lenny Moore, Jim Parker, Raymond Berry, Gino Marchetti, Big Daddy Lipscomb, et. al., were a perennial power. The result was that the Redskins lost virtually every time in contests that were regarded as a virtual joke by the Colts and a source of demoralization to the Redskins.

Other Marshall actions added to the torpid state of affairs. During training camp prior to the 1956 season, the team's leading rusher of 1955, Vic Janowicz, suffered a major traffic accident. He was thrown from a car, slammed into a tree, and incurred major brain damage. Janowicz's football career was over. The team was in a state of grief over him, and Marshall added to the despair. With a straight face, he actually announced that the accident had occurred outside of "company time," that he and the Redskins bore no responsibility in regard to the accident, and that he was not going to do anything other than simply cut Janowicz from the team payroll like any other player in camp who did not earn a spot on the team. The press was obviously not charitable toward Marshall here. The Redskins players themselves pooled money to help Janowicz and his family, and with every penny given they detested their owner all the more for his absurdly obdurate, some thought senile, and obviously parsimonious actions. (Chicago Bears owner George Halas may have learned from this, as nine years later the notoriously tightfisted Halas was remarkably supportive when two of his players—Willie Galimore and Bo Farrington— were killed in an auto accident prior to the 1964 season. Halas did everything he could for the two players' families, and with his actions the spirit of Chicago's players and fans rallied tremendously.)

While Marshall's views about personnel and race policies may not have resonated well among many of his players, he paid not the slightest heed. Instead, much like contemporaneous small Southern communities that clung ever more tenaciously to Jim Crow sensibilities as the world around them was changing, Marshall sealed himself within a world of friends and fans who felt a perverse camaraderie as the last of the old guard, the "lone wolf in lily-whiteism," as one reporter termed it.[4]

Elsewhere in sports, similar developments were occurring. College basketball fans in Kentucky, for example, were behaving much like some Redskins fans. At the University of Kentucky, coach Adolph Rupp refused to have any black players on his team and avoided playing teams, especially intra-state rival Louisville, which had integrated. In 1965 Rupp's all-white Kentucky squad would lose an NCAA championship game to an all-black team from Texas Western, now the University of Texas at El Paso. Still Rupp did not change his ways, and when he retired in 1971, Kentucky had yet to have a black player on its basketball team. Rupp was vilified in the press for his unchanging ways, and opposing team fans booed him incessantly, but in Kentucky many fans rallied around him. As a song writer of the era wrote: "He may be a fool, but he's our fool."

The Old South had been full of poor whites who were willing to take time away from their farms to help patrol and hunt down runaways for their richer slave-holding neighbors. Such action made no sense economically, as there was no pay for the patrol work, and the time away from their land further limited the farmers' incomes, many of whom lived in utter poverty. But the poor farmers acted as they did anyway. In the 1950s and early '60s, many of their descendents harassed Civil Rights workers, voted for George Wallace, and rooted for the Washington Redskins. Psychologists point out that when people engage in behavior that at one level they know to be illogical, yet persist in doing so anyway, there has to be a powerful force within them that compels them to do what they do in spite of all outer logic. As the compulsion resists logic, it will then grow even more resistant and turn vicious when logical and/or moral efforts are brought to bear from the outside to induce change. Among the Old South farmers, racism and a sense of racial and regional camaraderie (the origins of good ole' boy systems) were the obvious keys. While the stakes were much more precious, Marshall's true followers among Redskins fans showed much the same pattern. The "prosperity" of their world was crumbling as team losses mounted. Logic and the less racist patterns of their competitors showed an obvious open road to better times. Yet that road was not to be taken, and any who counseled that such a road be followed was immediately cast out of "the club." With an aging man like Marshall, there was an added feature of personally diminishing horizons that tightened his clinging to old ways and impoverishing all around him. In his youth, Marshall was a man of often interesting ideas and innovations. Now he was content to cling to his self-image and resist change at every turn.

It was amidst such a world of racial change and vehement resistance that the nation elected a new President in 1960. The Civil Rights Movement had been gathering momentum, especially since 1954 and the famous Brown v. Board of Education Decision. With President Eisenhower, who, with the Brown v. Board of Education Decision, was appalled that he had appointed Earl Warren to the Court ("the biggest damned-fool mistake I ever made"), the Federal government had been cautiously supportive. At first, the election of John Kennedy did not signal any great change in the nation's mood about Civil Rights, as Kennedy had been the moderate among the chief Democrats who sought the party's nomination. (Lyndon Johnson was the right wing's choice, Hubert Humphrey and Adlai Stevenson were the choices of the liberals.) Perhaps scandalized by the extremism and violence of some Southern racists' (as well as FBI Director J. Edgar Hoover's) resistance to Civil Rights activists, perhaps ennobled by a sense of higher duties once he took the office, perhaps pushed by an ennobled brother, Attorney General Robert Kennedy (who was certainly upset with J. Edgar Hoover in many ways), the Kennedy administration gave at least a better show of support to the Civil Rights Movement.

It remains a debate among historians as to how deeply committed John F. Kennedy was to the cause of Civil Rights. As he did not achieve much legislatively, was he merely interested in taking a more visible stance via verbal support? Alternatively, did he hold genuinely sincere, moral positions and take things with Congress as far as he could? Was, then, his successor, Lyndon Johnson, able to achieve much more because of the ground work laid by Kennedy, by Kennedy's martyrdom, by Johnson's political skills, and by a friendly Congress and resounding Presidential mandate rendered by the voters in 1964? These questions as to the true Kennedy legacy remain a matter of open debate among historians.

Whether motivated by image consciousness or by sincere idealism, Kennedy and many of his administration were interested in making visible strides on behalf of racial integration. Where Kennedy could act unilaterally, he provided some important symbols. Back in the 1930s, Eleanor Roosevelt had resigned from the Daughters of the American Revolution when the DAR refused to let contralto Marian Anderson sing at Constitution Hall in Washington. The FDR administration then saw to it that Anderson sang at an even more visible location—in front of the Lincoln Memorial. In 1961 Kennedy invited her to perform at his Inauguration. Members of the Administration resigned from various D.C. clubs which allowed no black members. Schools and labor unions received messages of advice against the continuation of past practices of racial discrimination. Hispanic-American farm workers organizer Cesar Chavez received an invitation to visit the White House. When it came to constructing and passing meaty legislation to ensure constitutional rights, however, the Kennedy administration was less successful. Kennedy's hold over Southern conservatives in his own party was not strong, and various conservative figures in the Federal bureaucracy, like J. Edgar Hoover, and in Congress, like Georgia Senator Richard Russell, were interested in blocking his efforts wherever possible. Whenever such conservative figures stepped forward, they felt little fear from their young, inexperienced President.

The racism within Washington, D.C. had never been effectively controlled or checked by the Congressional Committee governing the District of Columbia. That Committee had been dominated by Southerners anyway. Nevertheless, in the 1950s there had been some progress in the integration of some public facilities and schools. Some movie theaters, children's playgrounds, swimming pools, public golf courses, hotels, and restaurants had integrated; so did Constitution Hall, an especially poignant change in view of the earlier snubbing of Marian Anderson. Various professional schools in medicine, dentistry, and law remained segregated. (Here the old doctrine of "separate but equal" had in certain respects actually served African Americans effectively, as Howard University's professional schools were as good as those across town at George Washington and Georgetown. In 1960 fully half the African American doctors in the United States were products of Howard University.) There was some, albeit meager, progress in the hiring of African Americans in the federal bureaucracy, in Washington, D.C. hospitals, and in the police and fire departments, although few African Americans held positions of significant power and responsibility. With white flight to the Virginia and Maryland suburbs in the 1950s, the white/black composition of the District grew to a 50-50 level.

While this change was slow, all the changes marked contrasts to the steadfast Redskins. Baseball's Washington Senators had black players—both the old Senators club that moved to Minneapolis in 1961 and the "new" Washington Senators that formed the following season (now the Texas Rangers). In the NFL, 143 African Americans had played from 1946 to 1960; 83 African Americans were playing in the NFL in 1961. By any measure of comparison, Marshall's intransigence was absurd, and his stance was anything but a hidden little matter of concern to no one. Jokes abounded among the city's sports fans. (Question: What does "NAACP" stand for in the mind of George Preston Marshall? Answer: "Never, Anytime Any Colored Players.") Journalists in various African-American newspapers attacked Marshall. Sam Lacy of the Baltimore *Afro-American* wrote that, while he never favored anyone committing suicide, "in GPM's case, it would be forgivable."

Writers in the white press also attacked Marshall. Shirley Povich of the *Washington Post* declared Marshall "an anachronism, as out of date as the drop kick." Surveying the vast quantity of African American football stars, and noting that many could have been drafted by the lowly Washington Redskins, reporters pounded away at Marshall's absurd attitudes. They just did not make any sense in regard to the basic goal of a sports team—winning.[5] With changes occurring (albeit slowly) in the nation and in the city of Washington, and with at least a rhetorical commitment to civil rights, the Kennedy administration began to throw its weight against old George Preston Marshall.

When the Supreme Court was considering the Brown v. Board of Education case in 1954, they received a "friend of the court" brief from the State Department. The brief pointed out that the government, especially the State Department, was working very hard in the nation's efforts to win the hearts and minds of people in Third World nations to keep them and their governments from tilting toward the Soviet Union. In this context, the State Department pointed out to the Court that it was highly embarrassing for the country to have diplomats and trade representatives from African nations be subject to Jim Crow rules when they did something as mundane as board a bus in Washington, D.C. The linkage here of deeply patriotic anti-communist views to the cause of Civil Rights was something that divided the political right in America. The "red necks" of the South were, of course, vehement anti-communists, but they did not adjust their social outlooks. In the 1950s and early '60s, however, much of the more urbane right wing did shift, however slowly. For the Kennedy administration, this combination of Cold Warriorism and Civil Rights activism was easy. Some have seen a contradiction between the President's Civil Rights postures and his "Harry Truman with a Harvard accent" foreign policy. Yet the two combined quite easily for him, as well as for others in his administration, especially when a convenient little target like old George Preston Marshall could be caught between the cross hairs.

Stewart Udall had been a member of the House of Representatives from 1954 to 1960. There, he and Senator John Kennedy had become friends. The two were the same age, and Kennedy respected Udall's efforts on behalf of various causes that were part of the Democratic party's liberal wing—labor, civil rights, education, natural resource and environmental protection. Especially because of Udall's environmental and natural resource commitments, Kennedy named him as his Secretary of Interior. Udall's attorneys at the Interior Department raised to him the means by which the Department could place pressure on the little matter of George Preston Marshall and the integration of the Washington "Paleskins," as Udall would come to call them.[6]

Since the early twentieth century, Washington's baseball and football teams had been playing in old Griffith Stadium, built in 1901. In 1961 Federal money was being used to finance the construction of a new stadium. It was originally called D.C. Stadium. (After the assassination of Robert Kennedy in 1968, it was renamed RFK Stadium.) D.C. Stadium was constructed on the flatlands of Washington that border the Anacostia River, the tributary of the Potomac that runs through the city's East Side. Old Griffith Stadium lay to the north of Washington's downtown and east of Georgetown and fashionable Northwest communities, more in the poorer areas where the city's African American population resided. The new stadium lay ever more in the predominantly African American east side of the city. The notion of building a stadium so squarely in an African American neighborhood for a football team that was the only NFL club that was still all-white certainly held an altogether obnoxious air about it, one that ran counter to the poses of the new Kennedy administration. Such actions smacked of the bumptious, reactionary policies of figures like Governors George Wallace in Alabama and Ross Barnett in Mississippi. The Kennedy administration certainly did not want to find itself cast as indulging such reactionaries, even if the bier was so small as a mere sports team. The symbolism was important. Udall knew this and actually acted on his own, believing that the President and Robert Kennedy would favor his actions. Udall was right, about the Kennedys as well as in his policies.[7]

The Anacostia land on which D.C. Stadium was being constructed was part of the National Capital Parks System. There was the "hook" that gave Secretary Udall his opportunity. He wrote to Marshall in likely intentional abstract bureaucratic tone. Udall noted that Federal regulations forbade job discrimination by anyone using "any public facility in a park area." Noting "persistent allegations" that Marshall's "company practices discrimination in the hiring of its players," Udall advised Marshall to take heed "of the implications of this new regulation—and our view of its import." Udall took an additional step to add pressure by holding a press conference about the matter. This naturally drew significant media attention. Before the press, Udall spoke of the beautiful new stadium being built and how it ought to set "the highest of standards in terms of adhering to the policies of this Administration with regard to treating everyone in this country equally." His point was simple: if Marshall maintains his racist ban on black players with the Redskins, he would not be allowed to use the new D.C. Stadium. If Marshall "wants an argument," noted Udall, "he is going to have a moral argument with the President and with the Administration." Udall's warnings made front page news in the *Washington Post* and the *New York Times*.

Some contemporaries and historians have criticized the Kennedy administration for not achieving terribly much on civil rights and engaging largely in merely symbolic efforts on their behalf. A poll of historians conducted by the American Historical Association voted Kennedy one of the most overrated Presidents in American history, with the image versus reality contrast over his civil rights record being a major factor here. During Kennedy's time in the White House, such criticisms were raised as well. Indeed, explicitly in regard to the Redskins matter, Senator Kenneth Keating of New York commented ruefully on how the whole effort seemed a mere mask, a highly visible posture of commitment that shrouded an otherwise minimal record on substantial civil rights legislation: "I cannot help but feel that [Arkansas] Governor Faubus [the governor who sought to block the integration of public schools in Little Rock] and his cohorts need a little more attention than George Preston Marshall and Company. The Redskins may be [they weren't] tough on a football field, but the administration apparently has decided that they are easy targets in the political arena." Senator Keating was a Republican, one of the last of the generation of genuinely liberal Republicans who made up the GOP's so-called Rockefeller wing. Keating was thus both politically motivated against Democrats as well as honestly disturbed by the insincere posturing of some contemporary Democrats, such as the Kennedys, who personified "limousine liberalism" more fully than anyone else in the era. (In 1964 Keating would be the Republican opponent of Robert Kennedy in the New York Senate race, and in that election Keating would feel both frustrated and overwhelmed by a rush of sentiment for his opponent due to JFK's martyrdom, and by what he regarded as a misplaced sense of trust in the Democrats as the party with the best interests of the poor at heart, a mere image he felt had been largely manipulated from such *sui generis* efforts as those against the Redskins.) While Keating's motives in disparaging the Kennedys' efforts against George Preston Marshall may have been politically charged, F.L. Shuttlesworth, a reporter with the *Pittsburgh Courier*, also snorted a bit at Kennedy's offensive against the Redskins: "Where so little has been done for so long," Shuttlesworth wrote, "any little effort may appear to be large."[8]

While the Kennedys' motives showed a mix of sincere and ignoble politics, the Redskins case was certainly a delicious little morsel for the young administration. The Redskins' race policy was an absurd status-quo that was both indefensible and highly visible. Marshall could expect no support from the other NFL owners, even from the old guard who were still on hand, like George Halas in Chicago and Art Rooney in Pittsburgh. Nor would even the tiniest support come from the league's new young commissioner, Pete Rozelle, who was striving to cast himself as a kind of JFK figure within his little realm— a new generation of leadership in a new time. With Marshall completely on his own, Kenneth Keating had a point: the Redskins were an easy political target for the image-conscious Kennedys.

Like with anyone practicing an absurd old set of customs that made no inherent sense, Marshall's reactions to the Kennedy administration's pressure would involve a great deal of denial. Trying condescendingly to dust off such a young man as Kennedy, Marshall sniffed that if he met with the President, "I could handle him with words," noting, "I used to be able to handle his old man." While Marshall had made a lot of money in his laundry business in Boston, he was inflating himself when he implied that he was in the same league, verbally or financially, as Joseph Kennedy, Sr. Marshall was also deceiving himself about his ability to overwhelm such a figure as John Kennedy, as well as about how significant he was in the President's eyes anyway. John Kennedy never spoke about the Redskins issue. No reporter ever even raised it in a Presidential news conference. Kennedy left everything in the hands of Secretary Udall. Marshall was small potatoes, and Kennedy would have been doing Udall and himself a disservice had he addressed the matter directly. Marshall's thoughts of having any sort of meeting with the President of the United States were delusional. Kennedy was too shrewd to dignify an old codger like Marshall with an audience. Much of Washington Society had loved the Redskins for years, but that had not placed Marshall in anything close to a central spot in their political arena. Additionally, some major political figures, notably Secretary of Labor Arthur Goldberg, conspicuously cancelled their season tickets to the Redskins games because of Marshall's segregationist sentiments and policies. Marshall was about as important in Washington as the owners of the city's finest restaurants, and if any of them were under pressure to stop any racist practices in hiring and seating, Washington society would, with the exception of J. Edgar Hoover, go with the new political winds, and the matter would certainly not go to the Oval Office.[9]

Marshall's denials went further. He attempted to scoff about the matter to reporters: "I don't know what it's all about." Of course

Marshall knew exactly what it was all about. He was just refusing to recognize the severity of his past actions as well as the hurt they had engendered. Kenny Washington had less than a year to live at this point, but the squirming of Marshall, the man whose policies had help blackball him from the NFL back in 1940, must have brought a smile to his face. Showing further disingenuous efforts to push the issue away, Marshall nervously made attempts at humor with comments about how "We almost knocked Laos off the front pages." In mock consternation he posed, "I never realized so many fans were interested in a football team that won only one game."

In any such cases, points of response are obvious: Where a newspaper places a story about the Redskins or about a war in Laos is a matter for the editor. Whether the Redskins story is on the front or back page, the issue is still to be confronted. If Laos remained on the front page and the Redskins received no coverage, Marshall would have likely declared the matter to have no importance to the public; with keen press coverage, Marshall joked about the inappropriately high degree of concern. Whether the degree of public interest is massive or negligible, the legal and moral issues remained. Were any such counterpoints raised to a man like Marshall, he would have only countered with more clumsy evasions, likely focusing on allegations about the silly persistence of the person asking and re-asking the questions. Again, the counterpoint would be simple: the questions keep coming back because they must be addressed and were until then merely being evaded. Like many of Southern sensibility in these years, Marshall was in denial. He was too shrewd a politician to lose his temper like some old West Virginia Klansman, so he would try to use humor or any other sort of evasive tactic before the public and hope they would go along with him. Marshall's loyal supporters would naturally go along. But time was not on his side. The only question was how statesmanlike or crude would his ultimate reaction be.[10]

As the 1961 season approached, a few reactionary Redskin fans began to demonstrate. Signs were actually carried in front of the Redskins' offices with slogans like "Keep the Redskins White!" Some signs even displayed swastikas, and these were hardly counter-demonstrators. The American Nazi Party was actually involved here. Some even tried to argue that the involvement of the Federal Government in desegregating the Redskins may be part of a Communist conspiracy. It was always a hysterical ploy of many on the political right during the Civil Rights Movement (as well as in regard to the roughly contemporaneous protests over the Vietnam War) to link protests to the cause of communism and then summarily dismiss them. Thus the notion that the goals of people like Martin Luther King may be noble prompted a reaction to the effect that "the Devil hath the power to assume a pleasing shape." In regard to the Redskins, one opponent of integration wrote against government intervention and in defense of laissez-faire: "Once government sticks its icky fingers into free business, there is a hole in the line big enough for Mr. K[hrushchev] to smash through and rack up a winning score for his team." Well into the 1980s, South Africa's pro-apartheid leadership was regularly able to energize resistance to reform by claiming that the efforts to undo apartheid were but a veil for communism. In the early 1960s, the racist elements of the American political right, not terribly far removed from the days of Joe McCarthy, were anything but immune from such thinking. Any efforts here to ask how in the world the integration of the Washington Redskins could enable the Soviet Union to gain ground on the USA would not meet with much rational discourse.[11]

At this juncture, Marshall had an opportunity to step forth. He could have intoned noble words to the effect that "we have had our policies that may or may not have always been sound, but it is now time to move ahead as a team." He was certainly intelligent enough to make such intonations or to order an assistant to draft such words for him. (It would have been highly doubtful that anyone working for Marshall would have raised to him the suggestion of making such a statement. Marshall had run the team for nearly 30 years, and, as in any Jim Crow Southern town, his sensibilities could hardly be challenged from within.) Marshall, however, did nothing to discourage the "stay white" displays, even with Nazi symbols in the mix. It was as if he was somehow hoping that some miracle would occur and allow him to avoid confronting the reality that was staring him straight in the face. Like many old Southerners, he held fond memories of the old days, saw the Civil Rights Movement as an intrusion of outside agitators, and seemed to regard the irresistible pressures that were coming from the Interior Department either as part of a conspiracy or as some sort of bad dream from which he would somehow awaken. Like many right wingers of the day, Marshall clung to a perspective that much of the political left was merely a source of confusion for the nation. That way he need pay no heed to any of its forward-looking ideas. Always trying to make a posture of taking the whole matter lightly, Marshall quipped to one reporter: "You can't tell what will happen under the guise of liberalism."[12]

Various reactionary political figures, notably George Wallace, had been using anti–Federal Government rhetoric in their resistance to civil rights. Marshall's supporters did much the same, claiming, in addition to hailing the fear of communism, that it was wrong, no matter what the issue, for the government to step in and force the owner of any such privately owned business as a football team to do anything. Such arguments, of course, had and have little inherent logic. Does anyone believe, for example, that the IRS should have no enforcement power whatsoever? Marshall and his supporters made many arguments along these lines—about how they should be allowed to run their own affairs as they wished. Those who were already disposed to Marshall's views on race readily embraced this laissez-faire argument. Of course, the counter argument from the Federal Government could have been that if Marshall truly wanted no government involvement in his business, he should then build his own stadium on his own land. The specific contradictions here involving Federal favors for the rich never arose, for Marshall and friends were not interested in systematic argument. From "free market capitalism," to "communist plot," to the swastika, they were making whatever postures they could to drum up support. They were not going to get very far.

Racist segregationists continually prattled on with the self-deception that if only the Federal Government would stay out of their affairs, racial problems would somehow ease. The fact that such practices as slavery, lynching, and Jim Crow had never done anything but spread unless outside power interfered was simply something to be denied. Denial indeed seemed to be the order of the day. Meanwhile, Udall was not going to back down about the use of the new stadium in Anacostia. He told a reporter: "This guy's making a big mistake if he thinks our department is merely trying to get some publicity out of this thing."[13]

The NAACP was bringing other pressures to bear on Mr. Marshall. Throughout the 1950s and into the early 1960s, the Redskins scheduled pre-season games in Southern cities. This helped maintain the fan interest in the South for "their" NFL team. Ticket sales were almost always strong at these games, so Marshall had every reason to continue the practice. The problem was that many of the cities that hosted the pre-season games had been maintaining Jim Crow customs, and this included segregated seating in their sports stadiums. Two cities in Virginia, for example, Roanoke and Norfolk, had separate sections for African Americans in their sports arenas. Both cities regularly hosted Redskins pre-season games. Marshall did not care one whit about the separate seating. Doubtlessly, he favored it. But by the early 1960s there was not another NFL team that did not have black players. Here, then, the NAACP could exert pressure.

In August of 1961 the Baltimore Colts were slated to face the

Pittsburgh Steelers in Roanoke. The NAACP informed several African American players on the Colts and Steelers of the seating situation. They also informed the players and the press that they were filing a lawsuit over the city of Roanoke's use of municipal property (the stadium was owned by the city) for the promotion of discrimination and that there would be picket lines at the stadium on the day of the game. Various players, white and black, were hardly thrilled at the idea of crossing picket lines. The NAACP's pressure here worked in several respects. Many players expressed their displeasure. The press was covering the matter, increasing the pressure on other NFL clubs. The obnoxiousness of Marshall's stubborn refusals about integration thus grew all the more embarrassing in the eyes of other owners and in the eyes of NFL Commissioner Rozelle. The picket lines actually never had to go up in Roanoke, as Rozelle intervened and, through his influence, the segregated seating practices ended.

Later that month, Baltimore was to face the Redskins in Norfolk, Virginia. Norfolk also maintained segregated seating in its football stadium. That summer the NAACP bought up a block of seats in the white section and resold them to anyone who wanted them. Meanwhile, the Baltimore management spoke up, and among them was a former Colt player—Buddy Young—who was now the Assistant to the General Manager. In August of 1961, the Colts declared they would never again contract to play pre-season games in such situations where there is racial discrimination.[14]

Marshall and his supporters continued to sit still, however. They made noises about how there was no demand for equal representation on the Redskins for Puerto Ricans or people of other races. Marshall also asked why no one was asking any representation of women on the team. The Redskins put out other statements, asking, for example, about the racial composition of teams like the nearby (and all-white) U.S. Naval Academy and its use of D.C. Stadium. They asked about various theater and classical music organizations that used Constitution Hall. They also mentioned the White House, as it daily hosted the all-white White House Press Corps.[15] The Redskins were certainly showing to where their organizations rhetorical energies were devoting themselves. Further, while the Redskins may have had a point in their rejoinders, theirs was a response which, in effect, asked that all racial problems be solved at the same time, and that theirs, for some reason, be considered the sin of last correction. The solving of all a society's racial problems simply cannot occur simultaneously, and the law recognizes this fact. Like auto producers being pressured to come up with cleaner engines who say, "what about busses, trucks, and jet planes?" the answer is, "we have the right to make priorities, and we're dealing with your engines first." Perhaps one group or organization being singled out can feel the action to be unfair. People can respond to this perceived injustice in the courts, but the argument to the effect that "other problems have to be corrected first" never holds much water there, unless the judges possess similar sensibilities as those reactionaries appealing before them. Even accepting the Redskins' point of being unfairly singled out, the validity of the pressure for a correction of racial practices still stood, logically and legally. Most importantly, on the playing field the existing all-white Redskins team stank!

Amidst Marshall's verbal fencing, other pressures came to bear on him. Chicago White Sox baseball owner Bill Veeck stepped forward here. When owner of the Cleveland Indians in 1947, Veeck had signed Larry Doby and integrated the American League less than three months after Jackie Robinson broke in with the Dodgers. Apropos of George Preston Marshall, the always innovative Veeck made noises about creating a rival for Marshall in the form of a new, and integrated, American Football League club in Washington, D.C. Some Redskins stockholders, including future owner Jack Kent Cooke, took note of this threat. Ever more uncomfortable with the image they held in the sports world, Cooke and others urged Marshall to change his ways. Marshall still refused.

Increasingly embarrassed by Marshall's intransigence, the other NFL owners turned to the Commissioner's office. Just before the start of the 1961 season, Pete Rozelle met with Marshall and persuaded him to relent. Just before the opening of the 1961 season, Marshall made a public announcement in which he listed a number of players he wished to select for the Redskins in the next NFL college draft. On that list were some African American players, including the best collegiate running back of the time, Ernie Davis of Syracuse. In the 1961 season, the still white Redskins won a grand total of one game, lost twelve, and tied one. (Their one victory came on the last day of the season, and it was against the one-year-old Dallas Cowboys team, the Redskins' opponent in their only tie that season.) With the league's worst record, Washington was thus in a position to draft anyone they wanted. They chose Davis.

The fates would cruelly intervene in regard to Davis's future with the NFL. As it worked out, the Cleveland Browns strongly desired Davis to play for them. They traded an established star player to the Redskins for the rights to sign Davis. This player was Bobby Mitchell. Mitchell had shown an impatience and discomfort with Coach Paul

Brown's overbearingly controlling ways. Almost any player on the Browns who expressed such displeasure was going to be traded (Jim Brown was the only exception). In 1960 and 1961, quarterback Milt Plum had actually led all NFL quarterbacks in passing, the first quarterback to win the passing title in two successive seasons since 1942. But his impatience with Brown led him to be traded to Detroit. Bobby Mitchell had had many great games for Cleveland, but he was cast off to the Redskins. Jim Brown was successful because of his greatness and because a new owner in 1962, Art Modell, was willing to listen. It was Modell who fired Paul Brown after the 1962 season, and in the following year, Jim Brown set a new league rushing record which would not be broken until the season was lengthened.

With the trade of Mitchell to the Redskins, Ernie Davis was to go to the Browns, but in the summer of 1962, after playing with great discomfort in the College All-Star Game, he was diagnosed with leukemia. He never played again and died before the year was out. Meanwhile, Bobby Mitchell was a Redskin. Washington also received Leroy Jackson from Cleveland and traded with Pittsburgh for a guard named John Nisby. Additionally, they drafted two other African Americans from the college ranks—Joe Hernandez of the University of Arizona, who never signed, and Ron Hatcher from Michigan State. Jackson hardly played. Hatcher proved to be a good though hardly distinguished player. Nisby played well, but it was Bobby Mitchell who became a star flanker and runner, subsequently making the Hall of Fame. Led by Mitchell, the Redskins' 1962 record would improve to a more respectable 5–7–2. At the team gala in Washington prior to the opening game, the band was instructed to play "Dixie," as it had done for years. As the song began, Marshall yelled: "Bobby Mitchell, Sing!" Mitchell looked at the owner and smiled: "I'm sorry, Mr. Marshall," he chuckled, "I don't know the words." Mitchell's lithe wit always buoyed him throughout his career. Here he was able to finesse Marshall with ease, and there was little Marshall could do but fume to himself about it, particularly since Mitchell would play so well and be so popular with the fans. Elsewhere, Mitchell actually expressed respect for Marshall, stating that the main thing he always saw in Marshall was "a tremendous businessman." Mitchell was a shrewd "businessman" himself.

On the newly integrated Redskins, Mitchell and others had to dodge more than a few slurs and taunts. The Redskins players welcomed anyone with talent who could help their lowly club, but taunts from a few fans were downright mean. In 1962, D.C. Stadium had the most expensive seats in the NFL. The only cheap seats were those in the end zones close to field level. There sat many economically lower class whites, who were accustomed to watching a lousy team and felt entitled, especially among one another, to yell anything they wanted. Mitchell recalled that the taunts "affected me greatly—and I haven't forgotten them." John Nisby found little difference between the Washington fans and what he had found in Pittsburgh. Pittsburgh's fans, like Washington's, were used to watching a losing team. The open bigotry among the working classes of both cities was then acted out as a cultural rite, a kind of entitlement that was a consequence of steadily living with a poor team. Fans could bad mouth the team in football terms, and, like jokes in a redneck bar, the jump from there to racial slurs seemed minor to those accustomed to older mores. Mitchell had not seen any such behavior among the typical fans in Cleveland, who were accustomed to winning. Mitchell helped bring winning ways to Washington, but he had to endure much while doing it. The upper classes of Washington, D.C. may have held no less racist a set of sensibilities in their hearts, but their decorum kept them from the language of the cheap seats. Besides, they sat in the upper levels where the view was better, and their more "refined" thoughts were out of earshot of the players.

In 1962 Marshall actually invited Stewart Udall to the Redskins' opening home game. It was the third game of the season, and the Redskins were coming off an opening day tie with Dallas, in which Mitchell had run back a kickoff 92 yards for a touchdown, and off an upset win over a powerful Cleveland team, in which Mitchell had scored on a 50-yard pass reception at the end of the game. So team and fan spirit were up as the home opener against St. Louis approached. In the game, Mitchell again starred, catching two touchdown passes. From somewhere in the upper deck of D.C. Stadium, near Marshall's box, Udall heard a fan yell after Mitchell's first touchdown: "Thank God for Mr. Udall!"[16] Marshall said nothing.

During the fall season of 1963, Marshall suffered an incapacitating stroke. He relinquished control of the team to other stockholders, chiefly to Jack Kent Cooke and attorney Edward Bennett Williams. Marshall died in 1969, leaving a great deal of money for programs for disadvantaged youths in the Washington, D.C. area—he left explicit instructions in his will that the programs were to help children of all races. Marshall had begrudgingly yielded to the forces of integration. His stubbornness was one of the last major barriers to player integration in the NFL, but a hard road still lay ahead.

Thirteen

Back Down in the City of New Orleans

The road was still a tough one for African American stars like Bobby Mitchell, but it was certainly a different situation from that which crushed the ambitions of people like Joe Lillard, Ray Kemp, Ozzie Simmons, and Kenny Washington. In addition to the fact that teams in the NFL like Washington that avoided African American talent were doing so to their obvious peril, since they were simply turning good players over to their rivals, the NFL was dealing with an additional pressure to reform its customs. In the 1960s the NFL was involved in a decade-long struggle with a rival league, the American Football League. Back in the 1920s the NFL had successfully fought off challenges of rival leagues. In the 1940s there had been the major challenge of the All-American Football Conference, resulting in such teams as the Cleveland Browns, the Baltimore Colts, and the San Francisco 49ers eventually joining the NFL, but with everyone else folding. The NFL owners thus had reason to hope that in time the new AFL rivals would also fold, or perhaps find its best remnants absorbed into the older circuit. This had occurred with other rival leagues, but it would not happen here with the AFL.

Several reasons led the AFL to "stick." The major factor involved a combination of television and money. In its early years, the AFL fielded teams of clearly inferior quality to the NFL's. Nevertheless, the league survived and inched its way toward eventual parity. One by one, the major stars of the NFL retired. The pool of new talent from the college ranks was where the leagues' wars were fought, and here the AFL was successful in luring many talented young players. In their first year they signed the entire All-American backfield of 1959. The owners had the money to attract talent, and a key financial factor here stemmed from the fact that the NFL had an exclusive contract with

138

the Columbia Broadcasting System. The senior league could have, but chose not to, shared its game telecasts with other networks. The National Broadcasting Company, for a cheaper price, then bet that the football public would be willing to watch the other league's games too. NBC thus stuck with the AFL, and steadily infused it with money well beyond the meager revenues many clubs were receiving from ticket sales. This sole reliance on gate receipts (and a pittance from radio) had been the downfall of prior rivals to the NFL. Without television, the AFL probably would not have survived. In 1960 the average AFL game attendance was only 16,000. Some clubs, notably the New York Titans, nearly folded anyway. The television money was absolutely indispensable.

Forced to look for talent wherever they could find it, the issue of a player's race made no difference to most AFL scouts. Only one AFL location, Houston, posed any problems for players in regard to significant Jim Crow heritages and customs, and these problems were overcome. Six of the other seven locations of the original AFL—New York, Boston (now New England), Buffalo, Denver, Oakland, and Los Angeles (now San Diego)—presented few Jim Crow problems, nothing at least that the NFL cities did not face as well. The other original AFL city, Dallas, surprised many by being hospitable to the football players, white and black. (Nevertheless, after the 1962 season, due largely to rivalry with the NFL Cowboys, the AFL's original Dallas Texans moved to Kansas City to become the Chiefs.) In their searching for talent, it was the AFL that was most aggressive in seeking talent throughout the network of black colleges and universities. In earlier times, the heritage of Jim Crow could have been fatally damaging in regard to local customs and the ability to draw talent from all sources. For the AFL, the timing was fortuitous. African American talent could be brought into the league, and NBC's money could be utilized to pay everyone a competitive wage.

Amidst the AFL's struggles for survival in its early seasons, the status of African American players did at times become an issue. Some of Houston's local customs had to be addressed. And there was the issue of local customs in other Southern cities that came forth in some pre-season games. This problem of Southern resistance came roaring forth to confront the football world in January of 1965. It was a situation which could have been enormously destructive. As it was, many players' feelings were deeply hurt, but one city in the Deep South did have to take a hard look at itself and change some of its ways.

Starting in the 1961 season, the AFL scheduled an annual post-season All-Star game between its Eastern and Western conferences, as did the older NFL. NFL people snickered at the quality of play here, but the AFL simply had to bear the insults, for they knew that with NBC broadcasting the game, and doing so on a Sunday in January when there would be no other pro football on television, the football public would give their league a further look. From 1962 through 1964, the AFL All-Star games took place in San Diego (the city to which the Los Angeles Chargers had moved in 1961). The games won a large audience and were a financial success for the league.

In 1964 the AFL contracted with the city of New Orleans to have their next All-Star game held there on January 17, 1965. New Orleans was a football-loving town. They had such notable college teams in their region as Tulane and Louisiana State University, and every January 1 they hosted the Sugar Bowl. New Orleans's businessmen and political leaders dearly wanted a pro football team in their city and felt that hosting such a contest as the AFL All-Star game would make football people take further note of what a great, supportive sports town they had to offer. New Orleans leaders had formed the "New Orleans Sports and Cultural Activities Foundation, Inc." to go after such a contest as the AFL's All-Star game. Once the contracts for the staging of the game had been secured, the Foundation became the organization to handle all the game's local arrangements. The Foundation went to great lengths to advertise the game and promote ticket sales. By January 9, 1965, advance ticket sales had surpassed 50,000. This was a high figure for any sort of exhibition game, and for the AFL it was spectacular. The profits from the game were to go to the city's Police Foundation, but the real concern for New Orleans' business people was to demonstrate to America's pro football scions that the city was a good choice for the location of a new team.

With the game to occur on Sunday, January 17, 1965, players from the various AFL teams began arriving on Saturday, January 9. The league had arranged for hotels, the Roosevelt and the Fontainbleau, for all the players. They were to begin practicing on Sunday, January 10. On Sunday morning, many of the players arrived at the hotels' parking lots, prepared to board busses and head off to the practice field. To the surprise of the players and coaches assembled, about a third of the players did not arrive, and almost all the absentees were African Americans. Looking into the matter, coaches and AFL officials learned of a major problem.

A whole series of incidents had occurred over the weekend, events involving many African American players. At the New Orleans Moisant Airport, many African Americans could not get taxis to stop for them. The only black players who were able to get cabs were those who were arriving with white players. At the Fontainbleau and Roosevelt Hotels they encountered many racist remarks. Earl Fasion, a star defensive lineman with the San Diego Chargers, recalled standing in the hotel lobby and hearing one local ask another, in reference to him: "Is that Ernie Ladd?" (Ladd was another member of the San Diego Chargers.) Fasion heard the respondent in the conversation snap: "No, Ernie Ladd's a bigger Nigger than that. That Ladd is a big Nigger."[1] People like Fasion and Ladd were not about to put up with that sort of language.

The problems did not end with the airport and hotel lobbies. On Saturday evening, January 9, a group of players decided to go out to the New Orleans French Quarter. Some had trouble getting cabs at the hotel. A half-dozen cabs were apparently standing outside the hotel entry, and when the black players exited the hotel, all the cabbies got out of their cabs and walked away. Oakland Raiders running back Clem Daniels mentioned that one group of players actually stepped into the street and forced a cab to stop rather than run them down. "We jumped in," Daniels grimly recalled, "and the driver took us to our destination."

Once on Bourbon Street the players found several jazz clubs refusing them entry; even several African Americans who were accompanied by white teammates were turned away. At another club the whites were allowed in but the blacks were refused, so the whites left too. When they arrived at one club door, everything instantly grew quiet throughout the bar. The players were then informed they were not welcome. Walking to another club, they heard a motorist pass by and yell: "You Niggers get off the street. JFK's not playin' in here tonight." Finally, at the door of one club, a man actually drew a gun on them and yelled: "You Niggers are not coming in here." Fasion recalled that everyone in the group jumped back except for Ernie Ladd. Ladd stepped forth, and the gunman put the pistol right to Ladd's nose and promised: "I will pull the trigger!"

Some of the players feared some big trouble, not just from the gun-toting Louisianans, but from some of the players as well. San Diego Charger Dick Westmoreland recalled: "Some fellows, little guys at that, insulted us. Here I was with big men, Ladd's 320 pounds, and little guys were insulting us. But we didn't want trouble. I was worried because Ladd and Faison have tempers. I suggested we return to the hotel, and they agreed." Even when they tried to leave the Quarter, however, the players again could not get cabs. One cabbie told them there was a separate taxi company for blacks. When a player asked what that company was, the cabbie shot back: "Call one yourself; they are listed in the phone book." When a group finally caught a cab back from the French Quarter, the driver stopped six blocks from the Fontainbleau Hotel and told them he could take them no further and that they would have to walk the rest of the way. Some had to walk the whole way.[2]

Explaining such behavior on the part of New Orleans's citizens is, at one level, quite simple—racism. Yet at more subtle levels, the incidents reflected some of the dynamics that had been at work in the South (as well as elsewhere) for many generations. The city had always hosted the Sugar Bowl, and for years many of the participating college teams had had African American players. Just that month, Syracuse University had played in the Sugar Bowl, and their star fullback—Jim Nance—was African American. There had been no incidents.

It is possible that with all the publicity and promotional efforts from the city's politically powerful and economically wealthy scions, that many poorer people felt a kind of racism-induced betrayal. Historians of racism and slavery often noted how the institutions and habits did not make economic sense, particularly for the poorest whites, who willingly sacrificed to maintain the institution. The resulting "ole' boy" bonds of camaraderie between the poor and the rich whites had been the poor people's psychological compensation here. When challenges to Jim Crow inexorably grew in the 1950s and 1960s, especially when they gained more rhetorical support from such a wealthy white person as President John Kennedy, many poorer Southern whites resented it deeply and hatefully. They felt they were having something taken away from them which had given them status, a status for which they had been willing to sacrifice financially. Thus with the prospect of the wealthy classes in their midst growing richer, with the apparent further sacrifice of "old ways," there emerged an "Oh yeah, we'll see about that" attitude. While a few black college players arriving for the Sugar Bowl represented a mere annual visit, the arrival of a group of professionals symbolized the first wave of a possibly permanent change for which the wealthy were striving and which did not sit well with many common white folk. Historians of racism, like Winthrop Jordan, have speculated on the deeper Freudian dimensions in the fears that such huge athletes could denote—moving into the neighborhood, eyeing one's daughter—arousing phallic fears. It is speculative, but this could easily have been running through the anxieties of many subconsciences. The comments about such figures as Ernie Ladd, already known because he had been not just a football player but a professional wrestler as well, touched on the same dimensions that surrounded such a contemporary as Big Daddy Lipscomb. Fears, excitements, titillations, anger, resentment, they were all there, and they all came out at the airport, at the hotel, and in the streets and clubs of the French Quarter.

Beyond the psychological and historical dimensions at work in these events, the behavior of the cab drivers—all walking away from their cabs at the same time; one of them refusing to get within a few blocks of the Fontainbleau Hotel—certainly indicates that some planning had gone into the resistance. The fact that so many clubs reacted exactly the same way is a further indication of premeditation. The players certainly believed they had run into a planned resistance, and they were displeased, to say the very least.

Some of the players wanted to play the game in New Orleans anyway, as a kind of defiant protest, saying on the field "we're here in spite of you." Twenty-one AFL players* had other ideas. They wanted no part of New Orleans. Collectively they made up their minds that they were simply not going to play the game in the city. If they lost the fees they were to receive for their boycott, that was fine with them. Ron Mix, a white offensive lineman with San Diego, first leaned toward the idea of playing in New Orleans as a protest. But when he listened to the ideas, and even more to the angry tone, of his black teammates, he joined with them.

New Orleans officials learned of the incidents and quickly got busy trying frantically to patch matters up. They contacted all their friends who ran hotels, taxi services, and French Quarter Clubs and put them on alert. Nothing like this was to happen again. On Sunday afternoon the players met in the Roosevelt Hotel with some AFL league officials, with David Dixon, the head of the New Orleans Sports and Cultural Activities Foundation, and with other members of the Foundation. While it was not known until several days later, the President of the New Orleans Branch of the NAACP, Ernest N. Morial, also met with the players. Morial had actually counseled patience: "I asked them to wait and give us time, [hoping] we could have gotten public officials to have something done by the city government."[3] The players would not be moved, however.

Outside the meeting, Dixon expressed desperation: "We'll blow football [a further indication that the landing of a pro franchise was

---

The players were Cookie Gilchrist, Ernie Warlick, Elbert Dubenion, George Byrd, Larry Garron, Houston Antwine, Sherman Plunkett, Winston Hill, Sid Blanks, Art Powell, Clem Daniels, Abner Haynes, Mack Lee Hill, Julius "Buck" Buchanan, Bobby Bell, Dave Grayson, Frank Buncom, Dick Westmoreland, Willie Brown, Earl Faison, and Ernie Ladd.

on many minds] if they walk out. I have several prominent people in there talking to them." AFL President Joe Foss first wanted to try to smooth matters over, with Dixon still wanting to do anything to fix the situation.

The meeting in the Roosevelt Hotel was closed, but reporters were able to gather in the hall and could hear the discussions, which at times were rather loud. One of Dixon's colleagues said:

> We're asking you men to cooperate with us. This would be a deadly blow to our community, and it would undo all of the good that has been done in this area. We have arranged for you men to have access to all of the better class establishments—restaurants and night clubs— in the French Quarter. Why penalize all of these people because some discriminated against you?

The players remained adamant. In the meeting they responded (a New Orleans newspaperman actually prefaced the quotation by writing, "A Negro voice replied"): "You're asking us to sacrifice our principles and play when the conditions that surround us outside are deplorable. This is an unfair request." There would be no solution at the meeting. Some of the players wanted to stay and play, but they had agreed that if anyone still objected they would all leave. The players issued a statement:

> The American Football League is progressing in great strides and the Negro football players feel they are playing a vital role in the league's progression and have been treated fairly in all cities throughout the league.
> However, because of adverse conditions and discriminatory practices experienced by the Negro players while here in New Orleans, the players feel they cannot perform 100 per cent as expected in the All-Star game and be treated differently outside.

The players could have driven a selfish bargain with the New Orleans people and garnered several fun evenings in the French Quarter in the process. They could have pushed for greater financial compensation for their appearances in the game. But they were not going to be swayed. There would be no AFL All-Star game in New Orleans.[4]

To League Commissioner Joe Foss, the priority was the health of the League. He was not about to stage a game in New Orleans with half his players abandoning the effort. This would look terrible to the fans, and it could jeopardize his relationship with NBC, who still planned to televise the game and was not going to be pleased with substandard play. Foss had a solution: he moved the game to Houston. Everyone played. The stands were hardly filled, but NBC carried the game, and it reached the homes of millions of viewers.

As they faced abandonment, New Orleans officials were obviously upset. Revealing the true priority he and his colleagues had in mind, Dixon commented: "You can imagine what this will do to our efforts to bring professional football to New Orleans. I'm heartsick."[5]

In addition to being "heartsick," New Orleans officials had to do some serious stock-taking. Some journalists reacted with a bit of consternation. There was a pre-season professional football game in New Orleans in 1963 and two in 1964, during which there were no racial incidents. The Sugar Bowl had not had any racial incidents either. So why did this occur, they wondered. A Special Committee was formed, and they expressed regrets "'that a small number of unrelated incidents should imperil the good name of our city, which has made such extraordinary progress in race relations.'"[6]

What New Orleans officials had to take a long, hard look at were the psychological dimensions of racism that still pervaded the city, and the degree to which the laws that forbade racial discrimination in New Orleans were actually being followed. The stock-taking here was clumsy at best.

Likely, there was no nightly stream of racial abuse of the intensity that the AFL all-stars experienced on January 9. That was probably rooted in the simultaneous welling up of resentment from pockets of the city's poorer classes who felt that their psychological sense of racial superiority was now being sacrificed for the wealth of the city's blue bloods, especially since it was they, the poor white, who had sacrificed to place and keep the blue-bloods in power in the first place generations before. Such resentments had clearly surfaced on January 9, and they were hard to disentangle. Still, they had to be addressed.

Louisiana's Governor John J. McKeithen expressed regrets. H.T. Monte Shalett, the Chairman of the New Orleans Aviation Board, took up an investigation as to what had occurred at the Airport. The New Orleans Hotel Association, Restaurant Association, and Motion Picture Association all looked into the patterns of accommodations for all people at hotels, restaurants, clubs, and theaters.

While the brouhaha over the experiences of the AFL players caused some quick sympathetic reactions, some reactions were not so positive. Nicholas A. Tedesco, director of the city taxi cab bureau, did state that cab companies that carried white passengers were permitted "to carry Negroes, and a taxi cab issued a license to carry Negroes can carry white persons." But, Tedesco added, "we encourage them not to," because "if Negroes patronized cabs in large numbers which have permits to carry white passengers, it would injure the business of the Negro cab operators." Still, the largest cab company of New

Orleans issued instructions to drivers to pick up all prospective passengers whenever possible.

A real point of non-contrition came from the Mayor of New Orleans, Victor H. Shiro:

> If these men would play football only in cities where everybody loved them, they would all be out of a job today. Their reaction would only aggravate the very condition they are seeking, in time, to eliminate. … the players who walked out should have rolled with the punch. Almost all of them are educated, college men, who must be aware that you can not change human nature overnight. They have done themselves and their race a disservice by precipitous action. Not to mention the almost irreparable harm they inflicted on the future of professional football in New Orleans and the blow which they have dealt the distinguished citizens who were promoting the game.[7]

The indignance of such a figure as Mayor Shiro reflected the obdurate sensibilities of so many whites in regard not to the plight of a few football players but to the overall sufferings that had been going on all around them for generations. Like George Preston Marshall, people like Mayor Shiro harbored a sense of denial and felt that the only problems were being brought on by those who were agitating for change; and the main focus of Shiro's self-absorbed blubbering was on his wealthy friends who hadn't gotten what they wanted. The implication of Shiro's perspective was that positive change would come if people would just wait patiently for it to happen. When confronted with the historical silliness of such views, those who express them cannot normally be corrected via logic or facts.

Whether such sensibilities could have been disentangled if the All-Star game had come off in New Orleans is doubtful. Various people like the cab drivers could have felt that they had been able to act out their hatreds and pay no price for it. This could have emboldened further acts of hatred and sabotaged any other such efforts by city leaders as surrounded the staging of the All-Star game in the first place. With the players walking out, the city was left with little but shame. Those of well-meaning ideology could combine with those motivated by money to impose a stronger civic sense that such a shameful affair could not be allowed to occur again.

Even though the Mayor and many working class whites were not necessarily drawing many lessons from the incidents, the thoughtful people of the city had little choice but to take up the matter of enforcement of the existing codes that theoretically governed the practices of hotels, taxis, and clubs. This they did, and they did so rather effectively. The city "cleaned up its act," as concerted incidents of racial discrimination in clubs, restaurants, hotels, and taxis ceased. In the summers of 1965, 1966, and 1967, pre-season professional football games were staged without any racial incidents, as were more Sugar Bowls every January 1. In 1967 the city was awarded an NFL franchise, which continues to thrive in the city. Since then, New Orleans has hosted several Super Bowls.

It was a long process for New Orleans, and all other Southern (and Northern) cities, to extricate themselves from the entanglements which had confined them since the days of slavery and Jim Crow. For New Orleans, the events surrounding the abortive AFL All-Star game of 1965 and its aftermath played a significant role in unearthing some of the seamier sides of segregationism and racism. The incidents involving professional football had an impact well beyond the confines of its own game, for the city would never otherwise have had such a bright light of publicity exposing it, embarrassing it, and, above all, threatening it with severe financial losses. Sports was money, and money talks.

Fourteen

Point After

I believe that race relations between whites and blacks are better in the NFL than almost anywhere else in our society.
—*Tim Green*[1]

While incidents like those in New Orleans surrounding the 1965 American Football League All-Star game were enormous embarrassments, the AFL proceeded apace with their efforts to go after the best talent. Bit by bit they inched toward parity with the older NFL, and their mining the resources of the nation's historically African-American colleges was a significant part of this process.

Whether full parity with the older NFL was ever reached at any point in the 1960s remained debatable, but the two leagues did declare peace after the 1965 season. A common college player draft took place, ending the ruinous price wars for new players,* and an annual season-ending championship game commenced, later named the Super Bowl. The NFL champion Green Bay Packers demolished the AFL champion in the first two such games. Then in the famous third game the AFL champion New York Jets surprised the American sports world with a victory. Many felt the victory was a bit of a fluke. The following summer, that same Jets squad nearly lost to a College All-Star team. In the next year's Super Bowl after the 1969 season, however, the AFL Kansas City Chiefs convincingly overwhelmed the NFL Minnesota Vikings, and it was here that most serious football people recognized that the best of the AFL was indeed a match for the teams of the older league. Kansas City's victory was no mere fluke. It did not come with a bunch of oddly bounced passes, missed receiver sightings, and divert-

---

One source of difficulty beyond the large amount of money involved here was the fact that teams sometimes offered some rookies no-cut contracts, creating major resentments among veterans.

ing, New York–centered media hype. Kansas City was clearly a superior team, better than the Vikings and better than those Minnesota beat on the way to the final game.

One feature of Kansas City's victory among football analysts concerned the greater innovativeness of their offensive system. Through the early and mid–1960s, the NFL's leaders had giggled at the AFL's high scoring offenses, dismissing them as mere products of weak defenses and generally weak personnel through which a few strong-armed quarterbacks and light/fleet receivers could pass. At first, the older league's analysts were largely correct, but by the late 1960s the greater openness of the AFL teams to new ways and new ideas involved more complicated matters which should not have been cavalierly ignored. Kansas City's victory was then more of a true wake-up call to the older league, far more than was the previous year's victory, even though the Jets' win received more media hype due to it involving a New York team and a flamboyant quarterback.

Another significant feature of Kansas City's victory was the fact that the team was fifty percent African American. As in many institutions throughout the nation, professional football teams, after racially integrating, had employed quotas. Roosevelt Grier, for example, when a star defensive lineman for the New York Giants in the late 1950s, stated: "we knew only six black guys would make the team no matter how good they were."[2] (And there were only four African Americans on the 1958 Giants team.) No professional football team had ever achieved anything like 50 percent. With the Kansas City Chiefs organization this was not a matter of their seeking 50 percent as a goal, per se. One of their star players, middle linebacker Willie Lanier, commented that there was no offensive tokenism at work, no effort to push up the statistical presence of blacks for the sake of any sort of appearance. In 1968 there was little pressure for that anyway. Instead, there was, Lanier nodded, a simple "commitment to quality" on the part of the Kansas City organization.[3] It was with the recognition of such commitment, especially since it came with such stunning success, along with the changing political climate in the 1970s regarding race relations, that the walls truly began to crumble in regard to the heritages of racism in professional football. Ever more the norm for all players was a simple question: how good a player are you?

A certain paradox lay in the fact that it was in the 1970s that Affirmative Action also became fully institutionalized as a cornerstone in the administration of race relations in the nation. Up to that time, American conservatives had been, somewhat legitimately, tarred with the heritage of segregationist resistance to civil rights, from the general political activism of George Wallace to the recalcitrance of George Preston Marshall in football. It was in regard to Affirmative Action that many conservatives, as well as many traditional liberals, sprang to the offensive, claiming that any form of discrimination was wrong. Some may have been sincere and others disingenuous in their some-times newly articulated devotion to equanimity. Here the sports world provided such critics with evidence as to how far minorities could go in a meritocracy which held out but a fair field and no favor, and the example remains very much alive.

The American and National Football Leagues fully emerged in 1970. The strength of innovative teams like Kansas City compelled adjustments in coaching, personnel relations, and team cultures, and the distinctions between the old and the new league teams faded. Older teams from the NFL, Baltimore (now Indianapolis), Cleveland (now Baltimore), and Pittsburgh, were shifted from the National to the American "Conference." Inter-conference play was part of the regular season schedule, and African American players began to rise to wherever their talent would take them.

Throughout these final years of struggle for acceptance regardless of race, a sub-theme flowed throughout football, throughout virtually all sports, and throughout society at large. This concerned the race consciousness of many African Americans, which prompted an emphasis on racial differentiation, of essentialism as an element which, many argued, no African American could or should ignore. On the surface this seemed to mark an ironic contradiction. At professional football training camps in the 1940s and '50s, African American athletes first endured the indignities of having to eat and board separately. By the early and mid–1960s, some African American athletes were separating themselves with an air of defiance, especially in the dining rooms and in after-hours gatherings. In his last years as coach of the Cleveland Browns, Paul Brown noticed early signs of this. He saw that star running back Jim Brown was a leader here. Coach Brown did only one thing in response to this. He walked over to Jim Brown during a self-segregated meal and simply said: "Jim, don't do this."[4] Neither ever said another word to one another about the matter (and Jim Brown did not alter his ways). Many teams followed this example, although some teams of the 1960s did not. In Chicago, Gayle Sayers and Brian Piccolo, as rookies in 1965, became the first racially integrated roommates at training camp and during the season. Both players were quite successful, although each of their careers was cut short—Sayers's by a serious knee injury and Piccolo's by cancer, from which he tragically died. The best team of the decade, Vince Lombardi's Green Bay Packers, never had separations of players on the basis of race. Their lack of dissension was certainly part of their success.

The 1960s were a time in which people in many walks of life found themselves wrestling with the question of the degree to which various political issues took precedence over one's personal life and career. Football was no exception here, and matters of racial identity entered its corridors. It would take time to sort out the priorities. Cross-currents of varying, contradicting racial issues ran through professional football and through society at large amidst these years. On the one hand, many integrationists, white and black, saw such friendships as Sayers' and Piccolo's with great enthusiasm. The anthem of Martin Luther King's Southern Christian Leadership Conference, "We Shall Overcome," had, after all, the lyrics "Black and White Together, We Shall Overcome, Someday." Yet for others, different ideas were more important, and no matter the perspective, for many the issues were often more important than the mere instrumentality of an athletic endeavor.

Boxer Muhammad Ali sacrificed the very best years of his athletic career in service to his political convictions. No one else in professional sports would make that level of sacrifice, but many were willing to make racial issues a major priority while playing sports. In the decade of the 1970s, many athletes felt the "essentialist" emphasis on what distinguished the black race was as important, if not more, than the ideal of color blindness. Perhaps this was itself ironic in that the professional athletes had the wealth to indulge such fancies. But the essentialist dimension in African American political consciousness has a long history. Earlier in the twentieth century, Marcus Garvey had been one of the most vocal spokesmen of this theme of racial pride, and this came in conscious contrast to figures more devoted to integrationist ideals like the more conservative Booker T. Washington, or even in contrast to the more aggressive W.E.B. DuBois. In the 1960s various figures, most notably at first, Malcolm X, voiced a similar message, and he found that it resonated deeply among many African Americans, especially in the Northern urban areas of the nation. At the end of his short life, Malcolm X altered his views in favor of the ideals of color blindness, but, paradoxically, after he died his message of African American exceptionalism grew ever stronger, carried in various forms by such figures as Stokely Carmichael, H. Rap Brown, Bobby Seale, Eldridge Cleaver, and Huey P. Newton. The issue, and the tension, between the ideals of racial identity and race blindness remains very much alive. Because the issue of race consciousness had a definite vogue in the 1960s and early 1970s, it would inevitably affect any area in which African Americans played a significant role. Sports was thus anything but exempt. Given such heartfelt necessities of the era, it was difficult, if not impossible, for a man not to put racial issues ahead of any mere athletic endeavor.

While individual coaches and teams had different answers to the issue, some of the more successful teams of the 1970s, like the Pittsburgh Steelers, showed little in the way of racially exceptionalist politics. The Steelers were a team whose players had at least outwardly adopted the working class sensibilities of its city and local communities. This occurred in the wake of a decade in which America's blue collar population had symbolized much of the heart of conservative America—the so-called "Archie Bunker vote." In the '60s, blue collar America and its various labor unions had broken with the political left over issues like Vietnam and Civil Rights, where they had been notoriously resistant to integration, even to the point of violence, and vocal in support of such leaders as George Wallace and Lester Maddox. In general, blue collar Americans deeply resented the activism and lifestyles of the '60s Left, especially as it manifested itself among the youth. In 1970s Pittsburgh, these labor class folks then warmed to a football team which had been a loser for many years and which was appearing to respond to years of political unrest in the nation simply by hunkering down and doing its own job—they played football and that was it. As the blue collar economy of Pennsylvania and Ohio was in decay at this very time, a successful team—four championships in six years—also provided relief as well as a sense, however unrealistic, that the successful ways of an old economy, and an older society, could somehow return. Amidst such economic and psychological crosscurrents, the color of the skin of any star player hardly mattered as long as the athletes made little issue of it.

Pittsburgh's baseball team, the Pirates, performed in much the same manner and with the same social effect. The Pirates were the first Major League Baseball team to field nine black players at the same time, and they won two championships in the same decade. On both the Steelers and the Pirates there was little outspoken expression of *black* pride, just a lot of team and community pride. On both teams the personalities of various star players contributed further to community and biracial unity, eclipsing potential divisiveness. Outfielder Willie Stargell and defensive tackle Joe Greene endeared—and frightened—everyone equally, no matter their race. And Steelers' star running back Franco Harris, in addition to being a man of similarly inclusive nature, was himself half African American and half Italian

American. He attracted fanatical followings in both communities in the Pittsburgh area (and each were of considerable size). Each felt him to be one of their own. This marked quite a shift, given that the two communities were at virtual war with one another but a generation before when Mussolini invaded Ethiopia.

On many less successful teams the impact of race consciousness came forth, however. Where it engendered divisions among the players, the quality of team play often suffered. Beyond the troubling divisiveness, racially conscious behavior subtly—and not so subtly—changed the game. Players, acting in consciously race defining manners, altered the nature of the game's many practices and rituals. It was in the 1970s that special hand shakes, "high fives," "ball spiking," and the "in-your-face" type celebrations all entered the game, with many white players quickly picking up and imitating the new ways.

Until the late 1960s, players did little but shake hands or pat one another on the shoulder after a good play or a score. Indeed, the apex of football behavior, cemented by the cool demeanor of the two best offensive stars of the late 1950s and early 1960s, Jim Brown and Johnny Unitas, involved absolutely no on-field displays of emotion whatsoever. Brown once scoffed at the idea of demonstrably celebrating a touchdown, snorting: "That's what I get paid to do." But by the 1970s, and ever since, virtually every touchdown is a cause for revelry. With the new demonstrability of players, the League's leaders forged few policies in response to most of the new rituals, though a few extreme forms of celebration were outlawed as unsportsmanlike, even more so in the college game. Individual coaches and teams were generally free to do as they pleased. Some allowed free expression; some coaches sought to contain all such outbursts. Implicitly, the League allowed the market place of success to determine the best course.*

*One exception occurred during the Super Bowl of 1977. It had become an accepted and often-copied habit in that era for players, when they saw the television camera focus on them, to mouthe the words "Hi, Mom." In the week before the Super Bowl that year, players were told under no circumstances were they to mouthe those words. The betting parlors at Las Vegas that week then offered anyone bets on "the number of times players say 'Hi, Mom' on camera" during the Super Bowl. The parlors knew of the arrangement, and all amateur bettors who took that wager, unless they bet on "zero," were being suckered. Professional gamblers have not been able to destroy the game of football the way they nearly did baseball in 1919, but "Hi Mom" gave them a way to flex a bit of corrupt muscle. All players obeyed the order. It would have been an interesting situation had a star player broken ranks with one "Hi, Mom." A defiant player would have found himself blackballed.

Sometimes the matter of racial differences led to good humor. In the late 1960s, for example, the Los Angeles Rams boasted a superb defensive line which was called "The Fearsome Foursome."* The Four were so successful on the field and so hyped in the media that they became popular cultural and advertising icons. One of the players, Roosevelt Grier, was a reasonably good singer, and he persuaded his three teammates to do some performing with him as "the Fearsome Foursome." They were good enough and obviously of such fame that in the fall of 1967 they were invited to appear on a popular ABC music program of the day called *Shindig*. Grier sang the lead and the other three did the back up, much like such popular "Motown" groups of the day as the Temptations and the Four Tops. The problem was that the one white player of the Fearsome Foursome, Merlin Olson, very much a product of Utah State University, just could not learn, no matter how hard he tried, to do the various dance routines the rest of the group wanted to do. They could not leave Olson out of the group, so they had to reduce the dance background to the barest minimum, a level Olson could handle. The fact that Olson just could not dance became a source of neverending humor with the Los Angeles Rams team that season. Olsen earned a Pro Bowl appearance 14 times, and he made the Hall of Fame in his first year of eligibility, but he could not dance a lick.

While some of the perceptions of racial difference could be humorous, a potential tension in the issue lay in the fact that acts of racial consciousness could be felt negatively by others on the team, and this could lead to hostility, distrust, and dissension. This combined with the racial tensions that were still very much on hand in many communities where NFL teams existed and where African Americans were still seldom able to purchase homes in many neighborhoods. Such tensions were common in the NFL, as they were in a myriad of institutional settings in the nation at that time. These serious tensions were certainly more numerous and significant than any of the matter's humorous dimensions involving a player who cannot dance. Many white coaches were particularly concerned about divisiveness here.

Perhaps because they felt unduly threatened by matters of identifiably and self-consciously black behavior that lay outside their ken and control, many head coaches of the 1970s (and all were white) sought to clamp down on it. The seeming arbitrariness and insensitivity of this often backfired, as it usually engendered more resentment.

---

*The original Four were Merlin Olson, Roosevelt Grier, Lamar Lundy, and David "Deacon" Jones.

African American players found cultural outlets no matter the restrictions, and because of the restrictions the expressions assumed more pronounced auras of defiance and divisiveness.

The most successful coach of the latter quarter of the twentieth century, San Francisco's Bill Walsh, revealed an understanding of how the matter of race consciousness itself needed to be integrated into his coaching scheme. He hired the racially conscious sociologist Harry Edwards of the University of California at Berkeley to be a member of his staff, in effect recognizing the idea of race consciousness while conveying the clear message that any such demonstrations are not to be considered the least bit divisive in regard to the overall focus of the team, but instead be an integral part of the team's effort. Professor Harry Edwards had been a major intellectual source for several famous dissident African Americans in the late 1960s and 1970s. Many figures in American sports felt alarmed and threatened by Edwards, for he was a part of such actions as the fist-clenched demonstrations at the 1968 Olympics by 200-meter sprint gold and bronze medalists Tommy Smith and John Carlos. The alarm that some scions in American sports felt about Edwards may have been valid in regard to other figures, such as boxing promoter Don King, who cynically and narcissistically manipulated the "playing of the race card" as a means of attracting and conning various athletes, including Muhammad Ali and Mike Tyson. But Bill Walsh recognized in Harry Edwards not a con artist but a man of sincere intellectual convictions and substance. The two were able to work in concert. Their success underlined the point that race consciousness can be subtly combined with the theme of racial integration without contradiction or conflict. To say the least, not all other sports organizations or corporations have shown such wisdom as Walsh and Edwards, nor, not coincidentally, have they had the same levels of success.

Just as Al Campanis' famous 1987 gaffe about African Americans "lacking the necessities" to become major league baseball managers revealed there still to be a stubborn strain of racial stereotyping among the games scions, professional football has shown some of the same troublesome points. In 1983 CBS sportscaster Jimmy "the Greek" Snyder, in an obvious state of inebriation, was asked by some television reporters about why so many African Americans play professional football. Rather than state the fact that neither medical professionals nor sociologists nor anyone else can provide anything close to a good answer, beyond the simple point of the poorest having fewer outlets for their best to excel, Snyder launched into an utterly obnoxious and historically absurd tirade about how slave owners back in the eighteenth and nineteenth centuries bred the biggest and strongest slaves with one another to produce a bigger and stronger race. Television stations broadcast Snyder's ridiculous comments all over the nation. CBS fired him immediately, and Jimmy the Greek never worked in television again. (Most of his alleged insights into the game, which had largely to do with issues of point spreads and betting, had come largely from conversations with his friend Al Davis of the Oakland/Los Angeles Raiders anyway.) Still, his absurd mouthings were hurtful, to say the least. On another occasion, and during a national broadcast of a game no less, ABC's Howard Cosell, witnessing a pass reception by the Washington Redskins' Alvin Garrett, opined, "that little monkey can catch that ball." Cosell was not fired, but the embarrassing insensitivity of his comments was not lost on audiences. At the same time, O.J. Simpson, when working for ABC with Cosell, described one pass receiver's lack of jumping ability as "white man's disease." The term is a common one, used largely in basketball in regard to anyone who cannot jump well, but the question of whether such language belongs on national television is vexing. Where is a line of greater acceptability, or less offensiveness, drawn as one surveys the spectrum of comments from Snyder to Cosell to Simpson? Again, the question has never been fully answered, and perhaps it cannot be. Likely, a policy from the NFL or from television executives would only cause more problems, so such issues will continue to be addressed on a case by case basis.

Still, if such issues are the major remnant of the long heritage of racism and discrimination in professional football, one cannot but note the remarkable progress that has come in the game since the days of Fritz Pollard, Joe Lillard, Kenny Washington, Marion Motley, and George Preston Marshall. African Americans now dominate the National Football League's personnel. Traditional "white" positions, like defensive safety, middle linebacker, and especially quarterback, have ceased to be so racially defined. Coaching staffs, head coaching positions, team front office posts, and League management positions have all integrated. By the late twentieth and early twenty-first century a major strain of criticism of African American football players has been, in view of their wealth, that they need to be doing more to help African American communities.[5] It is a remarkable transformation, one over which some of the stars of previous times, like Fritz Pollard, lived to witness and chortle. Still, while it is a great transformation, it truly was, as the late Arthur Ashe eloquently noted, a most unnecessarily "hard road to glory."

Notes

One: The Early Days of Integration

1. Gregory Bond, "Whipped Curs and Real Men: Race, Manliness and Segregation of Organized Baseball in the Late Nineteenth Century," M.A. Thesis, University of Wisconsin, 1999.

2. See, for example, *Chicago Defender*, June 11, 1932.

Two: Early African Americans in Football

1. See Edwin Bancroft Henderson, *The Negro in Sports* (Washington, D.C.: Associated Publishers, 1939), pp. 86–96; Ocania Chalk, *Black College Sport* (New York: Dodd Mead and Co., 1976), pp. 140–60.

2. *Cleveland Gazette*, October 20, 1923; *Pittsburgh Post*, October 7, 1923.

3. Wendell Smith, *Pittsburgh Courier*, July 13, 1946.

4. See Henderson, *The Negro in Sports*, pp. 103–106.

5. *Ibid.*, pp. 92–4; Chalk, *Black College Sport*, pp. 171–75.

6. See, for example, *New York Times*, October 28, 1917, and November 5, 1918; see also, Henderson, *The Negro in Sports*, pp. 98–100; Chalk, *Black College Sport*, pp. 67–70.

7. William M. Tuttle, Jr., *Race Riot: Chicago in the Red Summer of 1919* (New York: Atheneum, 1970), *passim*.

8. *Atlanta Constitution*, January 2, 1929; *Los Angeles Times*, January 2, 1929.

Three: The Emerging Pro Game

1. David Neft, Roland T. Johnson, Richard M. Cohen, *The Sports Encyclopedia: Pro Football* (New York: Grosset & Dunlap, 1974), p. 17; Robert. B. van Alta, "Latrobe, Pa.: Cradle of Professional Football," *Professional Football Researchers Annual*, 1992, pp. 14–44.

Four: Ohio Football

1. Marc S. Maltby, "The Origins and Early Development of Professional Football," Ph.D. Dissertation, Ohio University, 1987; Milton Roberts and John

Seaburn, "The First Black Pro," *Akron Beacon Journal*, September 21, 1976; quoted in Charles K. Ross, *Outside the Lines: African Americans and the Integration of the National Football League* (New York: New York University Press, 1999), pp. 10–16; see also Keith McClellan, *The Sunday Game: At the Dawn of Professional Football* (Akron, Ohio: University of Akron Press), pp. 320–23.

2. Quoted in Tom Bennett, David Boss, Jim Campbell, Seymour Siwoff, Rick Smith, and John Wiebusch, *The NFL's Official Encyclopedic History of Professional Football* (New York: Macmillan Publishing Co., Inc., 1977), p. 15.

3. Quoted in Robert Smith, *Illustrated History of Pro Football* (New York: Madison Square Press, 1970), p. 220.

4. Arthur R. Ashe, *A Hard Road to Glory* (New York: Warner Books, 1988), p. 11; Ocania Chalk, *Pioneers of Black Sport* (New York: Dodd, Mead and Co., 1975), p. 212; Ross, *Outside the Lines*, p. 16.

5. Robert Smith, *Illustrated History*, p. 221.

Five: New League, New Opportunities

1. "Black Star Rising," NFL films, 1996.

2. Edna and Art Rust, *Illustrated History of the Black Athlete* (New York: Doubleday, 1985), pp. 228–29; Ross, *Outside the Lines*, p. 11; Greg Garber, "A Barrier Falls," *Football Legends* (New York: Friedman/Fairfax Publishers, 1993), p. 10. Garber claims that Rickey and Follis were not opponents but met as a result of being teammates on the football team of the Shelby (Ohio) Athletic Club in 1902.

3. *75 Seasons—The Complete Story of the National Football League, 1920–1995* (Atlanta: Turner Publishing, 1994), p. 24; Ross, *Outside the Lines*, p. 32.

4. John M. Carroll, Fritz Pollard, *Pioneer in Racial Advancement* (Urbana: University of Illinois Press, 1998), pp. 147–48.

5. Martin Bauml Duberman, Paul Robeson, *A Biography* (New York: Ballantine Books, 1989), pp. 34, 53–55.

6. Carroll, Fritz Pollard, pp. 178–79.

Six: The Curtain Falls

1. *The Oregon Statesman*, October 3, 1931, p. 6; *Oregon Journal*, October 3, 1931, V, p. 1.

2. *Los Angeles Times*, October 4, 1931, VI, p. 1.

3. *The Oregon Statesman*, October 15, 1931, p. 6.

4. *Los Angeles Times*, October 12, 1931, pp. 11–12.

5. *The Oregon Statesman*, October 9, 1931.

6. *Los Angeles Times*, October 12, 1931, p. 12.

7. *Oregon Daily Journal*, October 9, 1931, p. 14.

8. *Los Angeles Times*, October 12, 1931, p. 12.

9. *Oregon Daily Journal*, October 10, 1931, p. 8.

10. *Ibid.*, October 15, 1931.

11. *Chicago Herald* and *Examiner*, December 10, 1932, p. 19.

12. *Chicago Defender*, October 15, 1932, p. 8.

13. *Ibid.*, October 29, 1932, p. 8.

14. Thomas G. Smith, "Outside the Pale: The Exclusion of Blacks from the National Football League, 1934–1946," *Journal of Sport History, Vol. 15, No. 3* (Winter, 1988), p. 256; *Boston Globe*, October 17, 1932, p. 18; *Chicago Tribune*, October 17, 1932; see also Ociana Chalk, Black College Sport (New York: Dodd, Mead and Co., 1976), p. 227; and Ross, p. 40.

15. *Chicago Tribune*, October 24, 1932; Chalk, 227; Ross, 40.

16. Brooklyn Eagle, reprinted in *Chicago Defender*, November 23, 1935; see also Thomas Smith, "Outside the Pale," p. 258.

17. *Chicago Tribune*, November 21, 1932; see also Ross, *Outside the Lines*, pp. 39–44.

18. Charles Ross (*Outside the Lines*, p. 41) claims that the Cardinals had already suspended Lillard. However, the source of this dating appears to be a *Chicago Defender* article that was not published until December 10; *Chicago Defender*, December 10, 1932.

19. Al Monroe, *Chicago Defender*, November 12, December 3 and 10, 1932; quoted in Chalk, 228; Thomas Smith, "Outside the Pale," p. 256.

20. Bob Barnett, "Ray Kemp Blazed an Important Trail," Coffin Corner, Vol. 5 (December, 1983), pp. 3, 8; "Top Negro Stars in Pro Football," Sepia, Vol. 12 (November, 1963), p. 76; Thomas Smith, "Outside the Pale," p. 259.

21. *Pittsburgh Post Gazette* September 28, 1933, p. 17.

22. *Portsmouth Times*, October 2, 3, 1933.

23. *Cincinnati Enquirer*, October 9, 1933.

24. *Chicago Defender*, October 14, 1933, p. 8.

25. *Ibid.*, October 21, 1933.

26. *Ibid.*, October 14, 1933; Thomas Smith, "Outside the Pale," p. 257.

27. Dan Daly and Bob O'Donnell, *The Pro Football Chronicle* (New York: Collier Books, Macmillan Publishing Co., 1990), p. 114.

28. Thomas G. Smith, "Outside the Pale," pp. 256–59; Carroll, Fritz Pollard, pp. 144–45; Ross, *Outside the Lines*, p. 44.

29. Interview with Mary Grace Bassett, Washington, D.C., June 8, 2000.

Seven: The Segregation Years

1. Interview with Joshua Gibson, Jr., Slippery Rock, Pennsylvania, April 21, 2000.

2. *Chicago Defender*, December 14, 1935, quoted in Ross, *Outside the Lines*, p. 52.

3. *Chicago Defender*, October 27, 1928; Carroll, Fritz Pollard, p. 197; Ross, *Outside the Lines*, pp. 51–2.

4. *New York Amsterdam News*, July 30, 1938; Carroll, Fritz Pollard, p. 203; Ross, *Outside the Lines*, pp. 54–57.

5. *New York Times*, October 3, 1937, V, 1, 6.

6. *Philadelphia Inquirer*, November 26, 1937; see also Henderson, *The Negro in Sports*, pp. 117–121.

7. *Washington Star*, October 18, 1938, section A, p. 14.

8. See Henderson, *The Negro in Sports*, pp. 114–117.

9. *Chicago Defender*, October 27, November 4, 11, 1934; October 19, November 2, 23, 30, December 14, 1935; *Baltimore Afro-American*, November 17, 1934, October 24, December 5, 12, 1936; Ross, *Outside the Lines*, pp. 58–59; Carroll, Fritz Pollard, p. 271; Thomas Smith, "Outside the Pale," pp. 261–62.

10. *Chicago Defender*, September 17, 24, 1938; *Pittsburgh Courier*, Sep-

tember 10, 17, 1938; Thomas Smith, "Outside the Pale," p. 269; Ross, *Outside the Lines*, p. 60.

11. *Chicago Tribune*, September 24, 1938; *Pittsburgh Courier*, September 28, 1938.

Eight: Trials of the War Years

1. Oceania Chalk is one published source who claims that Dr. Drew died in an automobile accident; see Chalk, *Black College Sport*, p. 185.

2. Geoffrey Perrett, *Days of Sadness, Years of Triumph: The American People, 1939–1945* (New York: Coward, McCann and Geoghegan, 1973), p. 146.

Nine: The Early Saga of Marion Motley

1. The State, Columbia, South Carolina, October 3, 1939, p. 3; October 1, 1939, p. 4; *Atlanta Constitution*, October 14, 1939, p. 11.

2. *Cleveland Plain Dealer*, August 10, 1946, p. 14.

3. *Nevada State Journal*, September 20, 1940, p. 8.

4. *Ibid.*, September 22, 1940, p. 16; September 23, 1940, p. 5; October 12, 1940, p. 10; October 27, 1940, p. 5; *Salt Lake City Tribune*, September 28, 1940, p. 8.

5. *Nevada State Journal*, October 30, 1940, p. 10; November 1, 1940, p. 11; November 4, 1940, p. 10.

6. *Ibid.*, November 7, 1940, p. 8; November 8, 1940, p. 8; November 9, 1940, p. 11.

7. *Ibid.*, December 4, 1940, p. 8.

8. *San Francisco Examiner*, October 4, 1941, p. 5; *San Francisco Call Bulletin*, October 5, 1941, p. 6; *San Francisco News*, October 4, 1941, p. 4; *Nevada State Journal*, September 19, 1941, p. 8; October 3, 1941, p. 8; October 5, 1941, p. 33; October 21, 1941, p. 8.

9. *San Francisco Examiner*, October 4, 1941, p. 6.

10. *San Francisco Chronicle*, October 6, 1941, p. 7; *San Francisco Call Bulletin*, October 6, 1941, p. 5; *Nevada State Journal*, October 25, 1941, p. 8; November 9, 1941, p. 8; November 13, 1941, p. 8; November 14, 1941, p. 8; November 15, 1941, p. 8; December 5, 1941, p. 8.

11. *Nevada State Journal*, November 1, 1942, p. 1.

12. *Ibid.*, October 9, 1942, p. 3.

13. *Ibid.*, November 22, 1942, p. 8.

14. Paul Brown, with Jack Clary, *PB: The Paul Brown Story* (New York: Atheneum, 1979), 111–114.

15. *Ibid.*, 115.

16. *Lansing State Journal*, September 16, 1945, p. 26;

17. *Free Press*, September 16, 1945, section IV, p. 1.

18. Paul Brown, *Paul Brown*, 117.

19. *Chicago Tribune*, December 2, 1945.

20. Paul Brown, *Paul Brown*, 120.

Ten: The Walls Come Tumbling Down

1. *Pittsburgh Courier*, March 2, 1946.
2. Paul Brown, *Paul Brown*, p. 178.
3. *Pittsburgh Courier*, January 12, 1946, p. 14.
4. See Philip Berger, *Great Moments in Professional Football* (New York: Simon and Schuster, 1969), 41.
5. *Cleveland Plain Dealer*, August 9, 1946.
6. Berger, *Great Moments*, p. 41; see also Paul Brown, *Paul Brown*, p. 152.
7. Brown, *Paul Brown*, p. 129.
8. *Ibid.*
9. See Paul Zimmerman, "Strictly Personal: The Greatest Player," *The New Thinking Man's Guide to Pro Football* (New York: Simon and Schuster, [1971] 1984), p. 349.
10. Dan Daly and Bob O'Donnell, *The Pro Football Chronicle* (New York: Collier Books/Macmillan and Co., 1990), p. 118.
11. Greg Garber, "A Barrier Falls," *Football Legends*, p. 100.
12. *Pittsburgh Courier*, August 3, 1946, p. 16.
13. *Los Angeles Times*, March 21, 1946.
14. Quoted in Daly and O'Donnell, *The Pro Football Chronicle*, p. 118; *Pittsburgh Courier*, October 19, 1946, p. 14.
15. *Pittsburgh Courier*, October 19, 1946, p. 14.
16. Interview, *Sports Illustrated*, 1971; quoted in Ross, *Outside the Lines*, introduction; quoted also in "Black Star Rising," NFL Films.
17. Robert Smith, *Illustrated History of Pro Football*, p. 222.
18. Interview with Myron Cope, in Cope, *The Game That Was*, p. 254; "Black Star Rising," NFL Films, 1994.
19. Cope, p. 250.
20. *Ibid.*, pp. 250, 254.
21. *Ibid.*, p. 244.
22. Quoted in *Black Star Rising*.
23. *Ibid.*
24. NFL Films.

Eleven: The Life and Death of Big Daddy and the Decline of Marion Motley

1. See, for example, Farah Jasmine Griffin, *If You Can't Be Free, Be a Mystery: In Search of Billie Holiday* (New York: Free Press), passim.
2. William Nack, "The Ballad of Big Daddy," *Sports Illustrated*, January 11, 1999, pp. 70–86.
3. Interview with James Baker Donnelly, June 8, 1987.
4. See Nack, "Big Daddy," p. 78.
5. Cope, *The Game That Was*, p. 247.
6. Paul Brown, Paul Brown, p. 239.
7. Quoted in Paul Zimmerman, *Thinking Man's Guide to Pro Football*, p. 395.
8. *Ibid.*, p. 400.
9. *Ibid.*

10. Quoted in Cope, *The Game That Was*, p. 249.

11. *Pittsburgh Post-Gazette*, February 21, 2002, p. B-6, February 24, 2002, p. B-10; Butler (Pa.) *Eagle*, February 22, 2002, p. 6.

Twelve: George Marshall's Last Stand

1. Quoted in *Newsweek*, 60 (October 15, 1962), p. 99.

2. Bobby Mitchell, speech before Howard University Sports Symposium, "Griffith Stadium Memorial," Howard University Television (WHUT), March 30, 2002.

3. Paul Brown, *Paul Brown*, p. 193.

4. Sam Lacy, *Baltimore Afro-American*, October 8, 1960.

5. Sam Lacy, *Baltimore Afro-American*, October 22, 1960; quoted in Thomas G. Smith, "Civil Rights on the Gridiron: The Kennedy Administration and the Desegregation of the Washington Redskins," *Journal of Sport History, vol. 14, no. 2* (Summer 1987), p. 195; see also Ross, *Outside the Lines*, ch. 7.

6. Stewart L. Udall, interview with Thomas G. Smith, August 21, 1986, quoted in Smith, "Civil Rights on the Gridiron," p. 197.

7. Frank Barry, Solicitor, Department of Interior, memorandum for Stewart Udall, April 7, 1961; Stewart Udall Papers, box 90, University of Arizona Manuscripts Library; in Smith, "Civil Rights on the Gridiron," p. 197.

8. Quoted in the *Baltimore Afro-American*, May 13, 1961; *Pittsburgh Courier*, April 15, 1961; see also Smith, "Civil Rights on the Gridiron," p. 208.

9. *Washington Daily News*, March 26, 1961; see also Smith, "Civil Rights on the Gridiron," p. 200.

10. *Washington Daily News*, April 4, 1961; see also Smith, "Civil Rights on the Gridiron," p. 200.

11. Quoted in Smith, "Civil Rights on the Gridiron," p. 202.

12. *New York Herald Tribune*, July 14, 1961; quoted in Smith, "Civil Rights on the Gridiron," p. 201.

13. *Washington Post*, July 13, 1961; see also Smith, "Civil Rights on the Gridiron," p. 201.

14. *New Jersey Afro-American*, September 2, 1961; Ross, Outside the Lines, pp. 151–2.

15. Smith, p. 201.

16. Udall letter to Thomas Smith, May 25, 1985; Smith, "Civil Rights on the Gridiron," p. 207.

Thirteen: Down in the City of New Orleans

1. Quoted in "Black Star Rising," NFL Films.

2. *New Orleans Times-Picayune*, January 11, 1965; "Black Star Rising," NFL Films.

3. *New Orleans Times-Picayune*, January 11, 12, 1965.

4. Quoted *Ibid.*, January 11, 1965.

5. *Ibid.*

6. Quoted *Ibid.*, January 21, 1965.

7. *Ibid.*, January 12, 1965.

Fourteen: Point After

1. Tim Green, *The Dark Side of the Game: My Life in the NFL* (New York: Warner Books, Inc., 1996), p. 54.

2. Quoted in Daly and O'Donnell, *The Pro Football Chronicle*, p. 116.

3. "Black Star Rising," NFL Films.

4. Paul Brown, *PB*, p. 244.

5. See, for example, "Prisoner of Conscience," interview with Jim Brown, from jail, *Sports Illustrated*, April 15, 2002, pp. 54–57.

Bibliography

Books

Ashe, Arthur R. *A Hard Road to Glory: A History of the African-American Athlete 1919–1945*. New York: Warner Books, 1988.

Becker, Carl M. *Home and Away: The Rise and Fall of Professional Football on the Banks of the Ohio, 1919–1934*. Athens: Ohio University Press, 1998.

Bennett, Lerone. *Before the Mayflower*. New York: Penguin Books, 1982.

_____. *Wade in the Water: Great Moments in Black History*. Chicago: Johnson Publishing Co., 1979.

Bennett, Tom, David Boss, Jim Campbell, Seymour Siwoff, Rick Smith, and John Wiebusch. *The NFL's Official Encyclopedic History of Professional Football*. New York: Macmillan, 1977.

Billings, Robert. *Pro Football Digest*. Chicago: Follett Publishing Co., 1973.

Braunwart, Bob, and Bob Carroll. *The Alphabet Wars: The Birth of Professional Football, 1890–1892*. North Huntington, Pa.: Professional Football Researchers' Assoc., 1981.

Brown, Gene. *The Complete Book of Football*. New York: Arno Press, 1980.

Brown, Jim, with Myron Cope. *Off My Chest*. New York: Doubleday, Doran, 1964.

Brown, Jim, with Steven Delsohn. *Out of Bounds*. New York: Kensington Publishing Co., 1989.

Brown, Paul, with Jack Clary. *PB: The Paul Brown Story*. New York: Atheneum, 1979.

Camp, Walter. *American Football*. New York: Arno Press, [1898] 1974.

Capeci, Dominic J. *The Harlem Riot of 1943*. Philadelphia: Temple University Press, 1977.

Carroll, John M. *Fritz Pollard*. Urbana: University of Illinois Press, 1992.

_____. *The Hidden Game of Football*. New York: Warner Books, 1988.

_____, Michael Gershman, David Neft, and John Thorn. *Total Football II: The Official Encyclopedia of the National Football League*. New York: Harper Collins, 1999.

Chalk, Ociana. *Black College Sport*. New York: Dodd, Mead, 1976.

_____. *Pioneers of Black Sport*. New York: Dodd, Mead, and Co., 1975.

Cope, Myron. *The Game That Was: The Early Days of Pro Football*. New York: World, 1970.

Curran, Robert. *Pro Football's Rag Days*. Englewood Cliffs, N.J.: Prentice-Hall, 1969.

Daley, Arthur. *Pro Football's Hall of Fame: The Official Book*. Chicago: Quadrangle, 1963.

Dalfiume, Richard M. *Desegregation of the U.S. Armed Forces: Fighting on Two Fronts, 1939–1953*. Columbia: University of Missouri Press, 1969.

Danzig, Allison. *The History of American Football*. Englewood Cliffs, N.J.: Prentice-Hall, 1956.

_____. *Oh, How They Played the Game: The Early Days of Football and the Heroes Who Made It Great*. New York: Macmillan, 1971.

Duberman, Martin Bauml. *Paul Robeson*. New York: Alfred A. Knopf, 1989.

Edwards, Harry. *Sociology of Sports*. Homewood, Ill.: Dorsey Press, 1973.

Egerton, John. *Speak Now Against the Day*. Chapel Hill: University of North Carolina Press, 1995.

Evans, Arthur L. *Fifty Years of Football at Syracuse University, 1889–1939*. Norwood, Mass.: Plimpton Press, 1939.

Gaines, Kevin K. *Uplifting the Race*. Chapel Hill: University of North Carolina Press, 1996.

Garber, Angus G. *Football Legends*. New York: Friedman/Fairfax Publishers, 1993.

Garfinkel, Herbert. *When Negroes March*. Glencoe, Ill.: Free Press, 1959.

Gilliam, Dorothy Butler, *Paul Robeson, All American*. Washington, D.C.: New Republic Book Co., 1976.

Green, Tim. *The Dark Side of the Game: My Life in the NFL*. New York: Warner Books, 1996.

Henderson, Edwin Bancroft. *The Black Athlete: Emergence and Arrival*. New York: New York Publishers Co., 1969.

_____. *The Negro in Sports*. Washington, D.C.: Associated Publishers, 1939.

Herskowitz, Mickey. *The Golden Age of Football*. New York: Macmillan, 1974.

Hoyt, Edwin P. *Paul Robeson: The American Othello*. New York: World, 1967.

Hurd, Michael. *Black College Football, 1892–1992: One Hundred Years of History, Education, and Pride*. Virginia Beach, Va.: Donning Co., 1993.

Jones, Wallace, and Jim Washington. *Black Champions Challenge American Sports*. New York: David McKay, 1972.

Kaye, Ivan N. *Good Clean Violence: A History of College Football*. Philadelphia: Lippincott, 1973.

King, Joe. *Inside Pro Football*. Englewood Cliffs, N.J.: Prentice-Hall, 1958.

Klosinski, Emil. *Pro Football in the Days of Rockne*. New York: Carlton Press, 1970.

Leckie, Robert. *The Story of Football*. New York: Random House, 1969.

Leuthner, Stuart. *Iron Men: Bucko, Crazylegs, and the Boys Recall the Golden Days of Professional Football*. New York: Doubleday, 1988.

Maltby, Marc S. *The Origins and Early Development of Professional Football*. New York: Garland, 1997.

March, Harry. *Pro Football, Its Ups and Downs*. Albany, N.Y.: J.B. Lyon Co., 1934.

Mason, Nicholas. *Football! The Story of All the World's Football Games*. New York: Drake Publishers, 1975.

Mazón, Mauricio. *The Zoot-Suit Riots*. Austin: University of Texas Press, 1984.

McCalllum, John, and Charles H. Pearson. *College Football USA, 1869–1972*. New York: McGraw-Hill, 1972.

McClellan, Keith. *The Sunday Game: At the Dawn of Professional Football.* Akron, Ohio: University of Akron Press, 1998.

Morris, Aldon D. *The Origins of the Civil Rights Movement: Black Communities Organizing for Change.* New York: Free Press, 1984.

Muse, Benjamin. *The American Negro Revolution.* Bloomington: Indiana University Press, 1968.

Nazel, Joseph. *Paul Robeson: Biography of a Proud Man.* Los Angeles: Holloway House, 1980.

Neft, David S., Richard M. Cohen, and Rick Korch. *The Football Encyclopedia: The Complete, Year-by-Year History of Professional Football from 1892 to the Present.* New York: St. Martin's Press, 1994.

Nover, Douglas, and Lawrence Ziewacz. *The Games They Played: Sports in American History, 1865–1980.* Chicago: Nelson-Hall, 1983.

Perret, Geoffrey. *Days of Sadness, Years of Triumph: The American People, 1939–1945.* Madison: University of Wisconsin Press, [1973] 1985.

_____. *A Dream of Greatness: The American People, 1945–1963.* New York: Coward, McCann and Geoghegan, 1979.

_____. *There's a War to Be Won: The United States Army in World War II.* New York: Random House, 1991.

Peterson, James A. *Slater of Iowa.* Chicago: Hinkley and Schmitt, 1958.

Peterson, Robert. *Only the Ball Was White: A History of Legendary Black Players and All-Black Professional Teams.* New York: McGraw-Hill, 1970.

_____. *Pigskin: The Early Years of Pro Football.* New York: Oxford University Press, 1997.

Pope, Edwin. *Football's Greatest Coaches.* Atlanta: Turner and Love, 1956.

Powell, Harford. *Walter Camp, the Father of American Football: An Authorized Biography.* Freeport, N.Y.: Books for Libraries Press, [1926] 1970.

Ramden, Ronald. *Paul Robeson: The Man and His Mission.* London: Peter Owen, 1987.

Rathet, Mike. *From Out of the Huddle.* New York: Rutledge Books, 1970.

Reed, Merl. *Seedtime for the Modern Civil Rights Movement.* Baton Rouge: Louisiana State University Press, 1991.

Roberts, Howard. *The Story of Pro Football.* New York: Rand McNally, 1953.

Robeson, Eslanda (Goode). *Paul Robeson.* New York: Harper, 1930.

Ross, Charles K. *Outside the Lines.* New York: New York University Press, 1999.

Ruchames, Louis. *Race Jobs, and Politics.* New York: Columbia University Press, 1953.

Rust, Edna, and Art Rust. *Illustrated History of the Black Athlete.* New York: Doubleday, 1985.

Saylor, Roger B. *Scholastic Football in Southwestern Pennsylvania, 1892–1992.* Enola, Pa.: R.B. Saylor, 1983.

Smith, Robert. *Pro Football: The History of the Game and the Great Players.* Garden City, N.Y.: Doubleday, 1963.

Stagg, Amos Alonzo, and Wesley Stout. *Touchdown!* New York: Longmans, Green, 1927.

Stewart, Mark. *Football: A History of the Gridiron Game.* New York: Franklin-Watts, 1998.

Strode, Woody, and Sam Young. *Gold Dust.* Lanham, Md.: Madison Books, 1990.

Sullivan, George. *Pro Football A to Z.* New York: Winchester Press, 1975.

_____. *Pro Football's All-Time Greats: The Immortals in Pro Football's Hall of Fame*. New York: Henry Holt, 1968.

Sullivan, Patricia. *Days of Hope: Race and Democracy in the New Deal Era*. Chapel Hill: University of North Carolina Press, 1996.

Trent, Roger. *The Encyclopedia of Football*. South Brunswick, N.J.: A.S. Barnes, 1976.

Tumin, Melvin. *Desegregation: Resistance and Readiness*. Princeton, N.J.: Princeton University Press, 1958.

Tygiel, Jules. *Baseball's Great Experiment*. New York: Oxford University Press, 1983.

Vass, George. *George Halas and the Chicago Bears*. Chicago: Regnery Press, 1971.

Weyand, Alexander M. *American Football: Its History and Development*. New York: D. Appleton, 1926.

Whittingham, Richard. *Football Immortals*. New York: Macmillan, 1962.

_____. *What a Game They Played: An Inside Look at the Golden Era of Pro Football*. New York: Harper and Row, 1984.

Woodruff, Lorenzo Ferguson. *A History of Southern Football, 1890–1928*. Atlanta: Walter W. Brown, 1928.

Wright, David K. *Paul Robeson: Actor, Singer, Political Activist*. Springfield, N.J.: Enslow Publishers, 1998.

Wynn, Neil. *The Afro-American and the Second World War*. New York: Holmes and Meier, 1976.

Young, Andrew Sturgeon. *Negro Firsts in Sports*. Chicago: Johnson Publishing Co., 1963.

Zimmerman, Paul. *The New Thinking Man's Guide to Pro Football*. New York: Simon and Schuster, 1984.

Newspapers (Library of Congress)

Atlanta Constitution
Baltimore Afro-American
Chicago Defender
Chicago Tribune
Cleveland Gazette
Cleveland Plain Dealer
Des Moines Register
Detroit Free Press
Detroit News
Lansing State Journal
Los Angeles Times
Milwaukee Journal
Milwaukee Sentinel
Nevada State Journal
New Orleans Times Picayune
New York Times
New York World
Oregon Daily Journal
Oregon Statesman
Philadelphia Inquirer
Pittsburgh Courier
Pittsburgh Post Dispatch
Salt Lake City Tribune
San Francisco Chronicle
San Francisco Examiner
The State (Columbia, South Carolina)
Washington Post
Washington Star

Index